Florida – A Land Remembered

Patrick D. Smith

Cornelsen

Cornelsen English Library

Patrick D. Smith · Florida – A Land Remembered

Kurzfassung
Joachim Keferstein

Verlagsredaktion
Ralph Williams, Karin Wedepohl

Umschlaggestaltung
Heike Börner, Berlin

Titelbilder
Getty Images (© Joey Celis)
Corbis (© Emely/cultura)

Gestaltung & technische Umsetzung
Annika Preyhs für Buchgestaltung +, Berlin

www.cornelsen.de

1. Auflage, 1. Druck 2011

Alle Drucke dieser Auflage sind inhaltlich unverändert und können im Unterricht nebeneinander verwendet werden.

Druck: Drogowiec-PL Spolka z o. o., Kielce

ISBN 978-3-06-032952-6

Inhalt gedruckt auf säurefreiem Papier aus nachhaltiger Forstwirtschaft.

Contents

ONE

Florida
1863

"Damn! They have done it again!" Tobias MacIvey kicked the dry dirt away. His face was sweaty below his hat, and his slim six-foot body was dressed in a pair of old overalls.

Just then Zechariah MacIvey came out of the brush, running as fast as his six-year-old legs would carry him.

"What's the matter, Pappa? What is it?"

"The wild pigs have pushed through the fence again and got in the garden. Those devils ate everything. I guess we'll have to eat nuts like the squirrels ... But it looks as if the pigs can't be far away. Maybe we can get some meat out of it at least. Fetch my shotgun!"

A minute later the boy was back with the heavy shotgun.

Tobias took the shotgun and they followed the track carefully. Suddenly Tobias stopped and lifted the gun to his shoulder. Fifty feet ahead they could see seven pigs. Tobias pulled the trigger. There was a big bang followed by a cloud of smoke.

When they could see again, they heard the pigs squeaking loudly and saw them disappear, leaving one huge dead animal behind. They ran to it.

"You wait here," Tobias said. "And I'll get the oxen. This monster is over two hundred pounds heavy. We'll pull him back."

Tobias MacIvey was thirty years old. He had come south from Georgia in 1858 and had been living in Florida for five years. He'd arrived with just a horse-drawn wagon, a sack of corn, a sack of sweet potatoes, a few packets of seeds, and a shotgun. It had taken two long years to clear some land and build a house.

His wife, Emma, five years younger than him, and their baby had ridden behind him in a wagon.

Tobias had owned some land in Georgia. But the land couldn't feed the family. When he'd sold the hut and the land, he'd had just enough to buy what was in the wagon.

In Florida he swapped his horse for a pair of oxen which Zech called Tuck and Buck. He also got a small cow that would give them milk.

News of a coming civil war had been heard in Georgia, but Tobias hoped that the war would not reach Florida. There was nothing worth fighting over in the wilderness of Florida.

The first two years had been hard, with almost nothing to eat. Nothing much grew in the garden, and for hunting he needed bullets that he had no money for.

The first year, they lived in a shelter made of palm leaves. The second year, Tobias started building a house made of logs. Twelve months of sweat and pain went into the building before they could move in.

They did survive. Tobias learned everything by trial and error: how to build and how to grow plants. He caught raccoons and swapped their furs for an oil lamp so they could have light at night. Soap was made from animal fat and vegetables were dried for the winter.

The thing Tobias feared most were attacks by bears, panthers, and wolves. Nothing was safe from them. Night time was when they were most dangerous. So he kept the oxen locked overnight inside a small barn.

Tobias came into the clearing with the oxen and they pulled the pig back to the house.

Emma was a strong woman. She was used to hard work. Looking at the pig she said, "He's big but he's scrawny. I'll have to cook him well. Cut off some meat and I'll fry it for supper."

Late that afternoon they sat down to a meal. Tobias said, "Lord, thank you for this food, Amen." Then he said, "Ain't much to be thankful for, is it?"

"It's food," said Emma.

"But I would love to have some beef," said Tobias.

"Pig is fine for me, Pappa," Zech said, and helped himself to another piece.

They ate in silence for a moment.

"Everything will be alright in time," said Emma. "The Lord will look after us."

"We should start rounding up cows," said Tobias. "That'd help feed us, and we could sell them to make money too. Tomorrow I'll cut some cypress trees and start building a cow pen. And somehow or other I'm going to get me a dog and a horse."

TWO

Tobias was at the edge of the swamp early the next morning, cutting wood to build a fence with. Suddenly he noticed someone standing behind him. When he turned around he looked into the faces of two men and a woman. He saw that they were Indians and realized that they looked tired.

These were the first Seminoles Tobias had seen, one man called Keith Tiger, the other Bird Jumper. The woman's name was not mentioned. They were hungry and needed a place to rest.

"There's nothing here," Tobias said. "We have pig meat back in the house. We can feed you something if you go back there with me."

"There's not much time," Keith Tiger said. "There's a group of white men with horses and dogs following us, and they will be here soon."

Suddenly they heard barking dogs. Soon the white men came into the clearing. Tobias saw the guns on their saddles and shouted, "What the hell is going on here? You're on my private property!"

One of the men said, "It is against the law for an Indian to be in Florida now. They should be in Oklahoma."

Two of the men took their whips and started hitting the Indians.

Tobias shouted, "Stop, dammit! I say stop!" But the two men continued to hit the Indians.

Tobias took his shotgun quickly and fired, blowing one of the dogs in half.

"What the hell? That dog was worth as much as a horse!" one of them said.

"I told you to stop!" Tobias said angrily. "Now get the hell away from here, and don't come back!"

"You are taking up for the Indians? This ain't the end of this! We'll be back for sure!"

Tobias pointed the shotgun directly in the man's face. "You do, and it'll be the worst mistake you'll ever make!"

The three men left, and Tobias pointed his gun at them until they disappeared into the woods.

Later that afternoon Tobias and Zech sat on the ground outside the kitchen, watching the Indians eating hungrily, even breaking the pig bones with their teeth.

Keith Tiger drank the last drop of water from his bowl and said, "We thank you for this, Tobias MacIvey. I know no other white man who would have risked what you did for an Indian."

"We can't offer you much for your journey. I don't have a dog or a horse to round up cows," Tobias said.

"What you need is a marshtackie," Tiger said. "It is a small horse, but very strong and with a big heart. It can run all day and can take you in the swamps where no other horse can go. Perhaps you can catch one yourself. But now we have to leave, it is getting dark."

"It is no use leaving now. Stay the night and get a good rest in the kitchen," Tobias suggested.

"Thank you for the offer," Tiger replied. "We will not forget you for this. But we will sleep in the shed. We are not used to a house."

THREE

"You really have got to go, haven't you?" asked Emma.

"Yes," Tobias answered. "He's a state marshal. I got to help with moving a herd of cattle up to the Georgian border. It's for the army. It shouldn't take long."

"We'll be all right," said Emma, trying hard to sound brave. "We got meat, and there are enough vegetables."

"And I'll take care of the garden, Pappa," added Zech, who had been listening nearby.

Tobias put his hand on the boy's shoulder. "Give your mamma all the help she needs. But there's another thing you'll have to do. Take care of the oxen, Tuck and Buck, and don't ever leave them outside the barn at night. Not ever!"

He took Emma's hand and pulled her to him. "I'll be back just as soon as I can." With that he turned and walked away quickly, following the marshal into the woods.

Three days later they reached the Alachua Savannah. Addler, the marshal, had found five more men. When they reached the edge of the Savannah, Tobias was overwhelmed at the size of the open prairie. "That's the biggest pasture I've ever seen," Tobias said to Addler. Then he saw the herd of 600 cows, all with huge horns.

Addler collected the men and gave each of them a rawhide whip. "After you learn to use this thing, there ain't no cow alive you can't move with it. We'll move the herd along the military road. But don't push them. Just let 'em walk along as slow as they want, and eat. They should not lose weight. And keep 'em out of the woods. Just remember one thing. These are wild swamp cows. They can take off like thunder and run a man and a horse flat. Now let's go to Georgia. There are a lot of hungry soldiers waiting for us."

On the first evening of the second week they came to an empty farmhouse. They drove the herd into the pen for the night and locked the gate.

It was midnight when the first cry of a wolf broke the silence. It was answered by another and another. Shortly after, the cries were coming from all sides of the pen.

"Wolves!" Addler jumped up quickly "Good God a'mighty, that's all we need! There ain't no way we can fight off the damned wolves in the dark. Each of you build a fire every twenty yards around the pen."

Soon the darkness was broken by the glare of glowing fires. Tobias was on the south side of the pen. Suddenly the fence flew into the air. He jumped his horse away quickly, barely avoiding the cows that rushed by.

"Go after them," Addler's voice screamed.

Tobias rushed with his horse into the darkness, following the sound of the hooves. After a wild three-mile ride he and the other men were able to slow the herd down.

The rest of the night, two men stayed awake while the others slept. The next morning they saw that the herd was complete and continued their way to Georgia.

It was on the fifth night after Tobias had left that Emma was woken up by the sound of the oxen kicking the barn wall. She and Zech went to the windows and looked out into the darkness.

"Something is scaring them," said Emma. Suddenly they heard the sound of growling.

"Bears!" Emma shouted. "They're trying to get in the barn. Oh Lord, Zech! I don't know what to do!"

"Pappa always said take fire," Zech said. "He said they're scared of fire."

Emma shouted, "We'll light the two pine torches and go outside. But if they come after us, run back in the house as fast as you can!"

With the torches in their hands they went into the yard. The bears were walking around the barn and scratching the door.

"They're hungry, Mamma. Maybe if we open the smokehouse they'll smell the meat and go after it."

"It's worth a try," said Emma and slowly made her way to the smokehouse and opened the door.

Both bears rushed over towards her. She turned around and around, scared, pushing her torch at them. Zech threw his torch away, ran inside and returned pulling the shotgun behind him.

He was unable to lift it, he was so small and the gun was so heavy, but he pulled it onto a barrel and pointed it at the nearest bear.

When he pulled the trigger, the shotgun flew out of his hands and he was knocked backward, falling over and over in the dirt.

The load hit the bear with such a force that it knocked him into the wall ten feet away. The tremendous boom scared the other bear away into the woods.

Emma and Zech ran into the house and looked through the window.

"Pappa put me in charge of the oxen." Zech said. "That bear better not come back here no more. He better not!"

Emma put her arm around him. "I love you Zech. And Tobias will be real proud of you!" She thought that he had missed his childhood and that he had had to grow up too soon.

It took Tobias two weeks to do the job and to make his way down the west bank of the St. Johns River to the trading post and then through the woods to his farm. He ate what he could get, a stolen chicken or some frog's legs that he fried on sticks.

When he entered the clearing, Emma and Zech came running out of the house. Emma was happy and Zech shouted, "I killed a bear, Pappa! Bears tried to get Tuck and Buck, but we wouldn't let them!" And then they told Tobias about the dangerous night.

"You're a good boy, Zech," Tobias said proudly. "I couldn't have done it better myself."

"Where did you get that whip, Pappa? Can I see it?" asked Zech.

"You can play with it if you want," Tobias answered.

"You must be hungry," said Emma. "I'll get some of the bear meat and some greens!"

As he sat alone at the table, he could hear the whip cracking. He got up and looked outside, watching as Zech cracked it almost as well as Addler could.

FOUR

one year later

Tobias had just hunted some squirrels when he noticed a horse and a rider in a Confederate uniform.

"I'm Captain Graham," said the rider. "We need your help."

Tobias remembered what Addler had told him and said, "I can't go in the army, I am a drover."

"I'm not here to recruit you. We need some help to cut logs for a fortification."

Tobias did not want to go with the captain, but when the captain told him that he was even authorized to shoot Tobias if he did not follow, he said good-bye to his family again and followed the captain into the woods.

For days and days they cut logs. One day when they were loading the logs onto a wagon, they were surprised by a huge troop of Federal soldiers who had come to attack the Confederates. Tobias was able to hide in the bushes of a nearby wood and witnessed the terrible slaughter just metres away. After a long, hard battle it became deadly quiet. The field was covered with bleeding bodies. Tobias stayed in his hiding place for another night, and when soldiers came to load the dead bodies onto their wagons, he knew it was time to turn home.

Not far from where he had hidden, he saw a horse with a dead rider still on it. Both had got stuck in the thick bushes. Tobias had the courage to go over to them – and when he saw that the soldier was really dead, he took away his gun, his pistol and the bags of bullets. "I might as well take your horse," Tobias said to the dead soldier. "It will be no use to you any more, and it will be a present from God for me out in the scrub."

When Tobias rode into the clearing, he could not believe what he saw. His house was no longer there, nor the barn, nor the smokehouse, just piles of ashes. Only the woodshed remained.

Emma emerged from a bush and Zech looked out from behind the shed.

Tobias jumped from the horse. "What has happened, Emma? What is all this?"

"They came a week ago, fifteen of them. When they left the next morning, they set fire to everything but the shed."

Zech said sadly, "They killed Tuck, Pappa. They cooked him and ate him right here in the yard. And they took Buck with them when they left."

"Damned Federal bastards!" Tobias shouted angrily.

"They weren't Federals," Emma said. "They were Confederate deserters, Tobias. Our own people! But they did us no harm."

"Damn them!" Tobias jumped up and walked over to the piles of ashes. "Ain't no man ever gonna do this to me again! Not ever! I'll kill the first one who tries!"

Some time later he went to Emma and said, "We gotta leave, Emma. We'll go further south. This time we'll go to a place where nobody can find us."

FIVE

Kissimmee River

1866 – two years later

Tobias was out in the woods with Zech looking for cows running free in the scrub. Suddenly he saw a cow right next to them. He kicked the horse and followed the cow. He did not get too far because the horse crashed him into the low hanging branches of the trees. When he got up from the dust, he shouted angrily, "This damn army horse doesn't know how to do nothing but run in a straight line! We'll never catch the cows till we get a horse that knows how to run around trees instead of into them!"

"Can I ride the horse on the way back?" Zech asked.

"Sure. I think my back is broken anyway," Tobias said and they both went back passing their new pen with one cow in it.

"It ain't much," said Tobias "but it's a start. We'll try again tomorrow."

Their new cabin was in a clearing on the east bank of Kissimmee River. Tobias had known at once when he saw this clearing that this was the isolated place he had been looking for. The nearest trading post was fifty miles away. Tobias had already been there and had heard that the southern Confederates had lost. The war was over.

He made a branding iron MCI for MacIvey, and burned the letters onto the side of his one cow. He built a small barn for the horse and a stronger fence around the cow pen.

SIX

six months later

Tobias had been to the trading post again. On the way back he met the three Indians that he had saved from being killed by white men the other day. He gave them some bullets that they needed for hunting. When they talked about cattle they told him that he would need a marshtackie to follow cows. They added that he should not fence the cows in, but let them graze wherever they found grass.

When he came home, Tobias went with Zech to the pen, opened the gate and let the cow run into the clearing. Then he ordered him to get the iron and they both went to find cows that they wanted to mark. But once more they realized that neither the horse nor their equipment was good enough for hunting cows.

Sadly they went home and talked about how they could become successful cattle ranchers.

It was a month later when Zech ran into the clearing shouting, "Come quick, Pappa! Hurry! Down to the cow pen!"

Tobias ran outside. When they arrived at the pen, he could not believe his eyes. There was a small black horse in the pen, on its back a McClellan saddle. Tied to the outside of the fence were two dogs, both tall and gray, they looked like wolves.

Zech jumped up and down with excitement. "Where did they come from, Pappa? Who brought them here?"

"Can't say," said Tobias. "But that's a marshtackie. They're the fastest horses I ever saw."

Zech ran into the pen, jumped onto the saddle and turned the horse around. "Look here, Pappa! He can turn quicker than a rabbit!"

They named the marshtackie Ishmael and the two dogs Pip and Nip.

When they came to the house, Zech galloping like a flash of lightning, Emma came out and shouted. "What is all this, Tobias?"

"Well, it looks like Christmas has finally come for us," said Tobias. "Let's go inside and talk about it."

They sat down in the kitchen.

"It must have been the Indians, Emma," Tobias said, putting his hands on hers. "It means more than you know. At least we got a chance now. Before this we didn't have no chance at all. We were fooling ourselves, me and Zech, and I knew it. But now we got a chance."

SEVEN

The two dogs ran straight to the bull, as if they knew exactly where they would find it. Nip rushed in and grabbed it by the nose, and Pip sank his teeth into its left leg. Tobias and Zech rode their horses to the place. Tobias jumped off the horse, grabbed it by the horns while Zech tied its legs with a rope. They started a fire for the iron and pressed it to the bull's side.

"We should build a pen down here and wait till we get five or six cows and then brand them," said Tobias.

"I'm sure that Nip and Pip could bring in cows themselves. They can make a cow go any way they want to," added Zech.

When they had let the bull free, the dogs ran off again and a short time later they were barking loudly.

"They have found another one already!" shouted Zech, jumping up.

They rode to the dogs but could not see any cows. The dogs were near a thick bush.

Tobias took the rifle and shouted, "Zech, take a stick and throw it into the bush. Whatever it is, it will come out. But be careful, don't go too close."

After Zech threw a stick into the bush, nothing happened for a moment. Then a black head looked out.

"Don't shoot me, Mister. And call off the wolves. I don't mean no harm."

Tobias and Zech were both so surprised they did nothing but stare. Then Zech called the dogs to him and held them. Tobias had still the rifle in his hand and shouted.

"Fellow, what the hell are you doing in there? I could have shot you! You can come out there. We won't do you any harm."

When the Negro stood up he was even taller than Tobias, and he looked strong. He was the blackest Negro Tobias had ever seen.

"You ain't got a little bit of food, have you? I ain't eaten since the day before yesterday," asked the man.

"We don't have anything here," said Tobias. "But we'll be glad to feed you. Where'd you come from, anyway?"

"Just to the south of Tallahassee," answered the man.

"Tallahassee?" Tobias repeated. "You mean you walked down here from Tallahassee? Let's go to the house quickly, you sure must be hungry, and tell us about yourself. By the way, I'm Tobias MacIvey, and that is my boy, Zech. Who are you?"

"Skillit, that's all I've ever been known as."

EIGHT

Tobias watched the Negro as he quickly ate the bowl of stewed squash and then a fried raccoon leg, bone and all. Emma watched too, thinking that he was about the hungriest man she had ever seen.

"Would you like more squash or the last piece of raccoon meat?" she asked.

"I sure would. I'd be right happy to eat another bowl. You're a fine cook, a fine one."

Zech was fascinated by the black man. He said, "Have you been a slave?"

"Zech!" Emma snapped. "Don't ask him a question like that. It's rude."

"It's all right. I have been a slave. I was born on a plantation in Georgia. My daddy and my granddaddy were slaves. When I was four I was sold to a man at Tallahassee and went to the farm there. I guess I'd still be a slave if it hadn't been for the war."

"What happened to you after the war?" Tobias asked.

"When the war ended they said all the black people were free, and we could do whatever we wanted. I took a little piece of land and built me a cabin on it, and then I started to farm. Had a fine garden. Wasn't long after that some men come to the house one night. Said they didn't want black men to build houses or run farms. They was all dressed in white sheets and had hoods over their faces. I told them I was supposed to be free and I didn't see how a garden could hurt anybody. They hit me good, whipped me like I ain't never been whipped before; they stamped down my garden with their horses, and set fire to the cabin."

"They whipped you with a whip?" asked Zech.

"They sure did."

"Where will you go from here?" asked Tobias.

"Don't know. Don't even know where I am now."

"I got an idea," said Tobias. "Why don't you stay here for a while? You could be a help to me and Zech. We couldn't pay you nothing, 'cause we ain't got nothing. But we could build you a little cabin to stay in. The garden should come in soon, and if you help me with the smokehouse, we'll kill us a cow."

"You mean you'd let me stay here?" Skillit asked, not sure he could believe what Tobias said.

"What do you say, Emma?" Tobias asked.

"It's fine with me. He would be a big help to you and Zech. And it's just as easy to cook for four as three."

"Will you stay?" Tobias asked.

"I sure will!" Skillit said, grinning and flashing his teeth. "I'm awful tired of just walking around. I'm beholden to you, Mister Tobias! And to you, Miss Emma! I never knew them wolves were doing me such a favour by putting me in those bushes."

"They aren't wolves," Zech said. "They're dogs!"

Zech wanted to go for a ride with Skillit and grabbed his arm. When he reached the door, Skillit turned and said. "Soon's we're back, we'll start on that smokehouse, Mister Tobias. It won't take us no time at all to build one."

Zech pulled him out the door saying, "Come on, Skillit! Come on!"

Tobias and Emma were both smiling.

NINE

Spring
1867

The MacIveys had started their first drive after Tobias had got advice from a man at the trading post to drive the cattle to the town of Punta Rassa further south to sell them.

It was afternoon when the sky in the west turned solid black. The wind increased and lightning flashed. Tobias rode to Skillit. "Must be a storm coming up from out over the ocean. Looks to be a good one. If this thunder keeps up, the cows will run in all four directions all at the same time."

When the sky over them became black, the wind increased, making the prairie grass flat. Skillit rode up to Tobias and shouted, "Just look at that, Mister Tobias. I ain't never seen anything like it, and I sure don't like the look of it."

Lots of small animals – foxes, rabbits, raccoons – were running together, enemies no longer, moving rapidly westward. The rain came now in a blinding sheet. So they both rode back where they thought the wagon was supposed to be.

Skillit rode close to Tobias. "This marsh is the lowest land we been on since we started the drive. There ain't no place for the water to run off. If it keeps on rainin' like this the whole place is goin' to turn into a lake!"

Tobias agreed. "But we can't turn back. It's too late. It's ten miles back to higher ground, and we'd never make it."

Skillit pointed south and said, "Yesterday afternoon when I was lookin' for the trail I saw an Indian mound, right over there. If we go there, we'll be out of the water. It's only a mile. We can look for the cows tomorrow."

The horses pulled the wagon against the wind and rain towards the mound. The wind had blown all protection for Emma and Zech away.

They tried to drive the wagon up the slope but the horses fell down. Finally they let them loose, led them upward to the top and tied them to the trees.

By now the rain was not rain but solid water and felt like a river rushing over them.

"I've never been so wet," said Emma. "I feel like my skin is being washed off."

Some hours later the rain stopped, and they all looked out over a vast lake stretching as far as they could see. Emma said, "The wagon, Tobias. Everything is gone. It's all ruined. The salt and the flour and the coffee and the lard. Everything."

"The cows too," Tobias said. "Ain't no way they could have got out of that alive. They have all ended up as buzzard meat."

"Maybe the Lord didn't mean for us to own them," Emma said. "Maybe He means for them to be wild and free, like the deer and the birds."

"This ain't the Lord's doing," Tobias said. "It was only a storm. We'll start again, but I'm damned if I'll spend another year getting cows out of swamps one at a time. This time we'll find a better way to do it."

Zech walked towards them and shouted, "The horses and the dogs are OK. But they seem to be very hungry."

"We're all going to be hungry before we get out of this. But we will survive," said Tobias. "It will take more than a storm to keep me from taking cows to Punta Rassa."

Tobias then turned to Skillit and said, "Are you still with us, Skillit? You want to try again?"

"I ain't going nowhere but with you, Mister Tobias. This is the only family I ever had, and ain't no storm goin' to take it away from me. I'm ready whenever you are."

TEN

Spring

1868 – one year later

Tobias stood by the gate of the pen, listening to the cracking of whips far in the distance. Then came a faint sound like the drone of bees, and he felt the ground tremble. He watched as the tiny black spots grew larger and formed a small herd of cows thundering straight toward him. When he could see their horns point upward, he opened the gate and moved quickly to the side of the pen.

Tobias was busy counting. "This sure beats one-on-one in the swamp. Must be over thirty this time."

"Let's get the cows marked," said Skillit. "We need to get to Punta Rassa and sell all these cows pretty soon, Mister Tobias. My old trousers are about to fall apart, and there ain't anything Miss Emma can do for them!"

When they reached the homestead later that afternoon Emma was at the cooking pot. Tobias said to her, "You figure we got enough of everything to make the trip? We'll be ready to leave soon."

Emma put down the spoon and sat at the table. "You know what worries me, Tobias. You do not really know the way to Punta Rassa. It could be a difficult journey. And it is only Skillit, you and Zech. Zech is tough but he is still a boy."

Tobias remained silent for a moment, and then he said, "You're right Emma, and I know it. It worries me too. We got over seven hundred cows. Lord, what would the three of us do if we ran into something like that pack of wolves?

But I don't know what else to do. We just got to sell the cows. It's our only chance."

"Why don't you find some help? There must be a lot of men somewhere who need work. We could pay them at the end of the drive. That would make them want to get the herd there as much as you."

Tobias smiled. "You know, Emma, you have got a lot more sense than me. The family would fall apart without you. You're the only MacIvey with brains. Except Zech. I'm as stupid as that army horse, running in a straight line without looking where I'm going."

Tobias found two men in Kissimmee who were willing to work for him. When they arrived at their house after a long ride, he introduced Frog and Bonzo to Emma and Zech. They stared at the two strangers but welcomed them in a friendly way.

Finally Emma said, "Are you men hungry? I fixed a big pot of hot stew."

Right then Skillit came out of his cabin.

Frog took one look and exclaimed, "God a'mighty! That's the biggest black man I ever seen!"

"His name is Skillit" Tobias said. "He's my right-hand man. You and Bonzo can sleep with him tonight."

"I ain't sleeping with no nigger," Bonzo said.

"If you don't like his being here, you can leave right now! And you should know that Skillit takes his meals at the table with us. So if you don't eat with Skillit, you don't eat at all. Any objections?"

"No, sir, pleased to meet you, Skillit," said Frog pleasantly, remembering what Emma had said about stew.

ELEVEN

The line of cattle stretched out over a quarter of a mile, moving slowly, the men and dogs were at the sides, the wagon in the rear. Frog had met someone who had told him that if they wanted to get to Punta Rassa, they had to cross the Kissimmee River at Fort Basinger.

When they reached the fort, Tobias paid two dollars to load the wagon on a small wooden boat. The cattle, horses and men swam.

They were two days past the river when a rider came across the plain and to the wagon. The man said, "My name's Sam Lowry. Where are you headed?"

"Punta Rassa."

"You want to buy some cows?"

"What do you mean?" Tobias responded.

"I've seen you coming. I farm mostly, but I got sixty-five cows. Ain't no way I can get them to market by myself. So I'll sell them to you for three dollars each."

Tobias calculated in his mind and said, "I don't have that much money on me. Tell you what I'll do, though. I'll take them and pay you on the way back."

"Well, I don't know about that. I wanted cash. How did I know you'll come back and pay me?"

"You've got the word of Tobias MacIvey," Tobias said firmly. "I've never broken my word to no man, and I'm not going to do it for sixty-five cows."

The man agreed and Tobias shook the man's hand. "It's done."

For three days they moved over a marsh flat just to the south of a dense swamp. It was shortly before midnight on the third day when Tobias was awakened by the sound of a whip cracking three times, a signal for danger.

Immediately he saddled his horse and joined Frog and Bonzo. Skillit and Zech also came fast.

Frog said, "I'm glad you got here this quick. Look there at the edge of the swamp! Wolves!"

The dark animals were coming slowly closer and closer.

"We got to keep them back," shouted Tobias. "Frog, you and Bonzo ride around the herd. Zech, you and Skillit go back to the wagon and turn the dogs loose. Then bring all the firewood we got back here. Me and Skillit will use torches, and Zech, you go to the herd and help out there. If the cows break, get out of the way and let 'em go. We'll round them up in the morning!"

At once Nip and Pip rushed through the yellow grass, barking, and stopped halfway between the wolves and the herd.

Tobias and Skillit then ran constantly, moving with the wolves, pushing fire forward when a dark form came close.

One wolf broke into the outside circle of the herd and caught one of the calves. Nip and Pip were on the wolf's back at once, teeth snapping, hair flying, biting chunks from the wolf and jumping back. Some of the cows broke away from the battle site and ran into the swamp. A death cry came from the wolf as the dogs ripped its throat open. It stumbled back towards the woods, leaving a trail of blood. The sad sound seemed to frighten the other wolves. They ran quickly to the edge of the woods and disappeared.

For two days they turned back east. At dawn of the third morning Tobias rode to the edge of the swamp alone.

At breakfast he told the others that he wanted to drive the cattle through the swamp to shorten their journey. The others hesitated but said to Tobias, "You're the boss."

They decided to take six cows and test the way. The dogs came with them. Soon they had reached the water. The cows hesitated and tried to run back. But the dogs forced them to go on.

Skillit said, "I don't like this, Mister Tobias. Something don't seem right about this place."

The dogs were now having to jump to stay above the water level. Suddenly the lead cow disappeared under water, and came up bellowing; Then it seemed that dynamite was being set off under the surface. There was violence everywhere.

"'Gators!" Tobias shouted. "Turn back! Turn back!"

Pip went straight ahead, heading for the cows that were in panic. Zech kicked Ishmael in the side and followed the dog, the water now almost over the saddle.

Tobias watched, frozen with fear. "No, Zech! No!"

Zech was able to grab the dog and pull him onto the saddle. Water exploded all around him. Then Zech was out of the deep water and the others followed him.

"You could have got killed, Zech!" shouted Tobias. "A dog ain't worth the chance you took!"

"I wasn't going to let no 'gator eat Pip, Pappa. I knew Ishmael could do it. I could feel it."

"Lord, what could have happened," sighed Tobias later.

Skillit said, "You want to go to the wagon and take a rest?"

"No! Get the herd started. We'll go as far east as we have to."

When they came to end of the swamp and turned westward, they came into open prairie land. Another farmer met them and asked them to take his one hundred and ten cows to Punta Rassa. Again Tobias convinced the man to trust him. The man was even able to tell them the way to Punta Rasa. It would be about five more days.

The night before they were supposed to reach the marketplace everyone seemed very quiet, as if they did not yet believe they had manged to reach their goal.

For a long time Tobias sat silently next to Emma.

She finally said, "Don't be too disappointed if this doesn't turn out right, Tobias. It's not the end of everything."

For a moment he made no answer, and then he said, "I was going to say the same thing to you. I'm not sure I know myself what it means. All those times me and Zech chased bony cows through the woods and didn't catch them, it wasn't the money. I want the money for you and Zech. For me, I guess I just been trying to prove myself. All my life when I tried to do something worth anything I never made it. Every time I try, it seems somebody burns it or floods it or kills it. Maybe this time the Lord won't throw a roadblock in front of me. But if He does, I'll just stumble over it and try again. I'm not ready to give up yet, no matter what happens tomorrow."

Emma reached up and kissed him. "You're the bravest man I've ever known," she said. "I'm proud of you, and Zech is too."

TWELVE

Tobias passed several large holding pens and then turned down a bad road leading to the waterfront. He passed two stores and saw a saloon, a blacksmith's and a stable – all in all not very impressive. Tobias was more than mildly disappointed. At the end of the street he saw a dock with two ships in it.

Several men were sitting on the porch of one store. Tobias asked them if they could tell him if anyone was buying cattle and they pointed to a house near the dock.

"You want to see Captain Hendry," one of them said.

Tobias told the captain and his men about his herd in front of the town and said, "It must be around eight hundred and fifty heads. All in good shape, about five hundred pounds each."

"That's the kind we need," said Hendry. "If they are really in good shape, we'll pay sixteen dollars a head."

Tobias' throat turned dry. Even after hearing it, he still could not believe that the cows were actually worth cash money.

"Sounds fair to me. When do you want to see them?"

He was told to drive the herd into one of the holding pens. There they would be inspected and counted.

"You better go to the store and buy a trunk to carry the money in," said Hendry when Tobias rushed out. When he reached the wagon, he was breathless. He jumped from the horse and shouted, "We done it! We done it! Sixteen dollars a head! Spanish gold!"

Skillit's eyes widened. "Holy shit!" he exclaimed loudly. Then he turned quickly to Emma and said, "Lordy, Miss

Emma, I'm sorry! I didn't mean to say that. It just came out."

"I almost said it myself," Emma answered. "Tell us what happened."

Tobias told them about the conversation with Captain Hendry. Then he got on his horse again and shouted, "Let's get it done. But walk 'em slow. They need to keep every pound they got."

Tobias sat in a chair in front of the desk, watching Hendry make figures with a pencil. "Well, MacIvey, you've got eight hundred and sixty-five head, all in good shape. That comes to thirteen thousand, eight hundred and forty dollars. You want to count all of the money?"

"No sir, Captain Hendry, that ain't necessary," Tobias replied, overwhelmed by the figures. "I trust you. But if you got one of the gold coins on you right now, I'd like to keep it separate. It's the first I ever earned."

"I'll buy a trunk," he added, "and we all need boots, and I want to invite everybody to a meal in the café. My boy's never been in a café."

It was an hour before noon when they all went to the café and had masses of chicken and eggs as if they had not had food for month.

"Mister Tobias," Skillit said, "this is worth all them floods and wolves and 'gators."

Tobias took the gold coin from his pocket and handed it to Zech.

"This is the first coin Captain Hendry gave me. I want you to have it, Zech, and keep it. If you don't ever spend it, you'll never be out of money like I have always been."

The four men put the trunk in the wagon and Tobias counted out the coins to Frog and Bonzo. Then Tobias bought boots, socks, trousers, shirts underwear and a felt hat for everybody. They did not have dresses so Emma got pants as well.

After everyone had new clothes, Tobias went to the clerk and whispered, "Have you got a cook stove?"

"Follow me," said the clerk, whispering too.

When they went into a storeroom, Tobias saw a giant iron stove that he knew Emma would love.

"Sold!" he said. "But it should be a surprise. We will pick it up tomorrow."

After they reached the campsite and built a fire, Emma started supper while Zech fed the dogs. Tobias was alone at the wagon with Skillit. Tobias said to him, "I wanted to wait till we got back out here to tell you this. Those sacks of gold in the trunk are worth a hundred and twenty-five dollars each. One sack is yours."

"Oh, Mister Tobias, you don't need to do that," Skillit said, shocked. "These clothes you bought me are enough. You've done enough for me already. If I could just have two or three coins."

"No. Without you, me and Zech could never have rounded up all the cows. And from now on, every time we sell a herd your share will be a dollar for each cow."

"Lord, Lord, Mister Tobias, I don't know what to say. What am I gonna do with all that money?"

He got on the wagon, opened one of the bags, took a handful of coins and let them drop back in the sack. "I never thought somethin' like this would ever happen to me. When you found me in them bushes I hadn't had nothin' to eat for a week but berries and roots. Now I got a belly full of fried chicken, new clothes and a sack full of gold. Lord God, Mister Tobias, you're the best white folks there's ever been!"

Frog and Bonzo came back carrying big bottles of rum and offered Tobias a drink.

"I don't drink that rotgut. I saw my daddy die on this stuff. If you want to turn all your money into stale piss, that's your business. I got other uses for mine. But I want to ask you if you want to stay on with us or not."

"Well, I don't know," Frog answered, "you and Miss Emma has been real good to us, and we'd like to know what you got in mind."

"If you want to join us permanent, I'll raise the pay to a dollar per day, all the time, not just on a drive. And for every cow you and Bonzo round up in the herd, you'll get a dollar a cow when we're selling them. You'll do the branding and cutting, and we'll keep the tab."

"Let me see if I got this straight," Frog said, scratching his head. "If me and Bonzo round up a hundred wild cows and put 'em in the herd, we'd get a hundred-dollar bonus? You got a deal, Mister MacIvey. Hell, we'll get every cow out of every swamp and prairie in Florida!"

"It ain't that easy," Tobias warned "Don't count your money before you get it."

In the morning Tobias and Skillit got the stove from the shop. It was so heavy that it caused the wagon wheels to cut deep into the sand. When they reached the camp, Emma came to the wagon and stared at them with her mouth open.

"What on earth, Tobias? Where'd you get the stove?"

"At the store. I bought it yesterday as a surprise for you. You like it?"

"Lordy yes! It's the prettiest one I've ever seen. I can hardly wait to try it out."

Tobias climbed into the wagon and put three lengths of stovepipe into the stove.

As soon as the wagon was loaded, they moved up the road to the ferry. The old men there looked curiously at their new clothes. When the men and horses had swum through the river and the wagon left the ferry, one old man looked back across the river and muttered, "Damn! I thought for sure it was a circus coming."

THIRTEEN

Spring

1875

"Hell!" Tobias shouted. "They done it again. These stupid cows have eaten my orange trees."

He pulled one tree out of the ground and threw it at one of the cows.

Tobias walked into the house. "That's the third time I've planted them," he complained to Emma.

"Why don't you keep the cows out or plant taller trees?" she asked.

"Taller trees! That's what I'll do. I'll send Skillit right away for another wagon load," Tobias said and rushed out.

Tobias had made four more drives into Punta Rassa, each one larger than the one before. He now had regular buying points along the trail, and his last herd had over three thousand cows in it. They had to fight wolves or bad weather, but there had been no disasters. His old horse had died and been replaced and he had bought oxen to pull the supply wagon. He had also bought orange trees, but saved the rest of the money and kept it in two trunks in the house. The money was just something to pile into the trunks for Tobias and his family. Their lifestyle had not changed at all.

Zech was now as tall as his father, whose hair and beard were turning grey.

Zech, Frog and Bonzo had filled the pen with about sixty cows. They were getting hungry after a hard day's work. Especially Frog and Bonzo, who got frustrated because they had nothing to eat.

"I've got an idea," said Frog. "We are not far away from Fort Drum. We could go over there and get some food and be back here not long after dark."

Zech felt bad about leaving the cows alone because he felt responsible, but finally he gave in and rode with them.

After buying their food and filling their empty stomachs, they heard there was a dance in the town. Again the two drivers managed to persuade Zech to stay a bit longer.

"Cows ain't everything," said Frog. "Just take it easy. We'll stay for a short time and then leave. You might enjoy it if you'd try."

While Frog and Bonzo were enjoying themselves dancing, Zech was sitting on the porch when a young girl turned towards him. She had red hair like fire that flowed past her shoulders, green eyes, and white skin not burned brown by prairie sun.

She said, "You look like you're not enjoying it. Don't you feel good?"

"Well, I … I …," Zech could not answer.

"I've never seen you here before. My name's Glenda Turner. What's yours?"

"Zech," he managed to say, "Zech MacIvey. We came in for food. We've got cows out on the prairie."

"You want to dance with me?"

Zech felt like something had got stuck in his throat. "I don't know how. I've never been to a dance."

So she invited him for a drink. When she brushed against him Zech immediately smelled a scent he had never known before. He breathed deeply, drawing the smell into his lungs, feeling a strange sensation inside making him giddy.

"How old are you?" she asked.

"I'm seventeen, going on eighteen," Zech said, waking up from the cloud of smell.

"I'm fourteen, but my mother says I look older. Do you think I look older than fourteen?"

"I don't know. I've never been around girls. Only my mamma. But you look fine to me."

When the music stopped, Zech actually wanted to leave but then he heard himself say, "You want to see my dogs? They look like wolves."

Glenda was fascinated by the dogs so Zech continued, "Do you want to see my horse too? His name is Ishmael, and he's a marshtackie." On an impulse he said, "You want to ride? We'll just go a short piece and come back."

"If you'll help me into the saddle?"

Zech picked her up gently and placed her in the saddle. Then he sat behind her reaching around her slim body.

The smell of her came to him even stronger. Her closeness overwhelmed him, making him forget the cows and Frog and Bonzo and even where he was.

When they came back to the store and the people and the screaming fiddle, he was back to reality.

"I've got to find Frog and Bonzo and go now. There are bears and wolves outside and the cows might be in danger."

"Will you be coming back soon?" she asked.

"I don't know. We'll take the cows to Punta Rassa soon. If I don't come back this summer I will in the fall."

He left and met the two drivers at a wagon. They had watched Zech and Glenda, and began making fun of him. Zech demanded to leave at once; so they got on their horses and followed him into the darkness of the prairie.

An hour later, before they even reached the pen, Zech noticed something was wrong.

He stopped just short of the rails and stared into the pen. It was empty.

"How the hell did they do that?" shouted Frog when he arrived at Zech. "I checked the gate myself and it was locked."

Zech felt guilty. "I've never lost a bunch of cows, for no reason at all. We have to find them. I'll put Nip and Pip on the trail. They will help us."

When they followed the tracks, the path lead into thick forest.

Zech was just about to call the dogs and turn back when it came: a boom. Pip's head flew off and rolled forward, spilling out blood.

Bullets hit the ground around Nip. He stopped quickly, tumbling over and over. Ishmael jumped sideways and bolted into a clump of palmetto. Zech fell from his saddle and onto the ground.

Frog shouted. "Bushwhackers! Stay hidden!"

Zech was unable to move first. Then, realizing what had happened to his dogs he jumped up and staggered forward. "Bastards!" he shouted. "Bastards!" He started to run, screaming.

Frog tackled him from behind and tried to hold him. "Don't be a fool, Zech! They will kill you as well!"

Zech gave up with tears in his eyes. They found Nip under a tree, unable to even lift his head.

Zech dropped to his knees. "He's been shot. But I can make him well!"

"No Zech," said Bonzo, "you got to finish him off. His guts are blown apart."

"I can't do it," he said and ran away. "You'll have to do it."

Later Zech insisted on burying the dogs and, with their hands, the men made a hole, laid the dogs in it and covered them with the soil.

"I ain't never been able to read the Book. If I could, I'd say words, but I don't know how. I hope the Lord blesses them."

"We don't even know who it was," said Frog. "And chances are we'll never know."

"I'll know. If I ever come on them, I'll know. Someday I'll find them."

"Don't try to blame all this on yourself, Zech," Tobias said after they had returned home. "It doesn't matter at all about the cows. We got plenty more. Staying for the dance might have saved your life!"

Tobias sat next to Zech and laid his arm around him. "Son, I know you're hurtin' now, hurtin' real bad. Don't be sad too long about Nip and Pip. What you have just seen and been through will come again and again. This whole wilderness is built like that, and it's going to get worse before it gets better.

I ain't good with words, you know that. All I'm trying to tell you is to be strong. Don't ever let nothing get you down. Don't be afraid or ashamed to love, or to be sad when the thing you love is gone. If you want to make it in the wilderness, you got to be strong."

"Yes, Pappa, I understand. And I'm sorry I cried for the dogs."

"Don't be. Don't ever be sorry for something like that. There ain't nothing wrong with a man crying. Now go to the barn and see to Ishmael."

Everyone was in the house at noon the next day, just finishing dinner, when the wagon drove into the clearing. It was full of orange trees. Skillit stopped just next the porch and shouted, "I'm back, everybody! I'm back! Come and see what I got!"

They all ran out and were surprised to see a girl on the wagon seat, sitting there like a frightened owl, her eyes wide and blinking.

Skillit said, "This is Pearlie Mae. A preacher married us, proper and legal. Mae'll be a big help to Miss Emma. She knows how to cook and wash and sew and do most things. You don't mind that I brought her here, do you? She won't be a problem to nobody."

"Of course I don't mind," Tobias replied. "You're most welcome, Pearlie Mae."

Frog started jumping up and down, shouting, "Yee-haw! Yee-haw! Old Skillit's got himself a woman! There's going to be little black babies all over the hammock, thick as junebugs!"

"Shut your mouth, Frog," Skillit said, "before I pick you up and throw you into a buzzard's nest where you belong!"

When she finally climbed down the wagon, Emma put her arm around the frightened girl and said, "We're glad to have you in the family, Pearlie Mae. Real glad. Let's go into the kitchen and have some woman talk and leave the men to themselves."

FOURTEEN

They were on another drive, when they saw two young Indians riding towards them on horseback. They asked for Tobias MacIvey and were sent to him.

"We were sent by my grandfather," one of them said to Tobias. "He wishes to buy some cows from you. During the long drought our cows have all died or gone away. So our people are dying of hunger and we have nothing to trade."

"I'm sorry to hear you are in such a fix. How many cows do you want?" asked Tobias.

"Just a few. We don't have any money but my grandfather will pay you as soon as he can."

He told Frog and Bonzo to select twelve of his best cows and gave them to the young men who had lots to talk about with Zech. He was so interested in their life and what they knew about dogs and horses. He was shocked when he heard that Indians were not allowed to herd cattle.

After a good meal that Emma had cooked, the Indians did not accept Zech's offer to come with them but took off alone.

For four more weeks the family stayed on the prairie, going wherever there was grass; then Tobias rode ahead and bought cows that were added to the herd. By the time they reached Punta Rassa, the herd was over three thousand. The price this time was 12 dollars per cow.

Tobias went to the store afterwards and the clerk called to him, "Mr. MacIvey, I almost forgot to tell you. We just got something that might interest you. It's the New Winchester repeater."

They went to the storeroom and the clerk took a rifle and handed it to Tobias. "Seventy bullets fit in the magazine. It will shoot as fast as you pump the lever!"

The price was fifty dollars. Tobias surprised the clerk and bought nine rifles and six cases of ammunition.

When they were about to leave the village, they passed one of the holding pens and suddenly froze in their saddles. Three of the cows had the mark MCI on their sides. They stopped at once to examine the other cows and found more with the same brand.

Four men were standing at the gate. Tobias rode to them and asked, "Who owns this herd?"

"I do," one of the men said. "How come you want to know?"

"Some of the cows in there have my mark. MCI. Where'd you get them?"

"Took them off some rustlers, over near Okeechobee. Some Indian boys. These bastards will steal anything they get their hands on!"

"What did you do with the boys?" Tobias asked.

"We hung them."

"You did what?"

"We hung them," repeated the man. "That's the only way you can teach Indians a lesson."

"I gave them the cows!" Tobias shouted, his face getting red, his hands trembling. "You killed the boys for nothing!" He took his whip and hit the men until Skillit stopped him.

One of the men tried to stand up, then dropped to his knees. He said weakly, "We'll get you for this, Mister. It ain't finished yet."

"If I ever see you again or if you come looking for me, I'll kill you right away," shouted Tobias, and rode away.

Tobias was still trembling when they left the place. Frog and Bonzo had taken out the cows with MCI and asked Tobias what they should do with them now.

"I'll drive them myself this time," he said. "I'll take them down to Okeechobee. The Indians told me that they would find me if I go there. I'll take Zech with me. Skillit, Frog and Bonzo will take care of Emma."

FIFTEEN

It was early the next morning when Tobias and Zech left the others to go to the Indian village. They had bought supplies and got directions from Captain Hendry.

On the fourth day they reached the western shore of the Okeechobee. There were too many trees along the river, so they chose another path and drove the cows slowly.

Tobias had problems staying awake on the saddle, but he refused to stop except at night.

One night when they were sitting by a fire, hoping the smoke would drive away the mosquitoes, a man stepped from the shadows.

"Do not be frightened," the man said. "I'm not armed. We have known you were coming this way for the last two days."

Tobias said, "My name is Tobias MacIvey and this is my son Zech. We're looking for the village of Keith Tiger."

"I am Tony Cypress, father of Willie Cypress. We know who you are. I will lead you to our village in the morning. But tell me, do you have news of my son and James Tiger?"

Tobias dared not tell him about the hanging of the two boys at this time. So he just answered, "We have seen them. We can talk of this tomorrow with you and Keith Tiger."

There were a dozen chickees in the village, small huts of cypress poles. Under one an old woman was stirring in a cooking pot with a wooden paddle. All of the men were dressed similar to Tony Cypress, and the women wore multicoloured ankle-length dresses.

Keith Tiger wanted to know where his grandson was but Tobias wanted to start differently. "The cattle are for your people, and we have brought gifts. Go and get them, Zech."

Zech went to the horses and returned in a moment, placing boxes on the ground and handing two rifles to Tobias. He passed them on to Keith Tiger and said, "These Winchesters will help your people."

Tiger was very thankful. "I thank you, Tobias. Bow and arrow are almost useless in the swamp. But why is it that you drive in the cattle and not James and Willie? What is your news of them?"

Tobias knew he had to tell them the truth now. He spoke slowly and told them the terrible news they had learned in Punta Rassa.

Both Indian men sat without moving, trying to take in the meaning of the words. Keith Tiger's eyes became wet as he said, "In my heart I was scared of this, but it hurts no less hearing it from you now. I hoped somehow they would return. This is the end of me. They killed my son in the last war, and now my grandson. It would be better if they came and killed me also. I have no reason now to live."

"If they ever come to my place, I'll kill them myself. This is my promise. I hope you don't blame me for what happened. If I had known, I would have ...," Tobias stopped speaking. He stood up suddenly, staggered a few steps and fell.

Zech hurried to him. He shook him and said, "Pappa! Pappa! What is it? What is the matter?"

Tobias shook as if cold, and sweat poured from his face. He tried to speak but couldn't, then he looked at Zech, begging for help.

Tiger put his hand on Tobias' forehead. "It is malaria. We have seen it many times." Then he turned to Tony Cypress. "Get the medicine man, and tell Lillie to bring blankets. Quickly! He is very sick!"

"Don't let him die," Zech begged.

Tiger put his arm around him and said, "The medicine man can help him more than anyone. He knows what to do. We will do all we can to save him."

For a day and a night Zech walked around the chickee, until Keith Tiger came to him and said, "There is no need for you to do this. Go and get food and rest. If there is a change, we will tell you."

He went to the far side of the clearing with some food that the old woman had given to him and he sat down on a log alone.

He didn't know that someone was coming closer.

"They will make your father well again," said the girl. She was sixteen, slim and firm, with black hair that swirled down to her hips. She had a thin mouth, high cheekbones and oriental eyes, the look of pure Seminole. She said, "I am Tawanda Cypress. Willie was my brother."

Zech said, "I'm sorry. I offered to ride with them but they wouldn't let me. If I had gone anyway, he would be here now."

"You don't know that's true. It's possible they would have killed you too just for being with James and Willie." Then she changed topic. "Would you like to see the great marsh?" she asked, trying to turn his mind to something other than Tobias. "I can show you."

Zech agreed, knowing that the medicine man would do his very best.

They had a wonderful time in the scrubs, and Zech fell in love with this marvellous Indian girl. She showed him a new world, one that he had dreamed of.

Back in the chickee, one of the cows had been killed and the smell of roasted beef was in the air. Tawanda prepared two wooden plates for them and Zech followed her to the edge of the clearing.

"We're breaking a Seminole rule," Tawanda said. "An Indian woman does not sit next to her man while eating."

"My mamma and pappa do everything together," said Zech. "It will be the same with us." He spoke as if they already belonged to each other. But it did not worry him. He felt as comfortable with her as he did with Ishmael.

They talked about their different worlds for a long time until she suddenly got up.

"I'd better go to the chickee now before my father comes looking for me. It is also against Indian rules for me to sit here with you in the darkness."

The next morning Tawanda fixed breakfast for him and he ate hungrily. Keith Tiger came to them and said. "Tobias will be fine now. He is over the worst. In a few days you will be able to take him home. I know your people are worried."

These words brought his mother into his mind. He felt guilty about not thinking of her earlier but was glad that he would be able to ride home with his father soon.

In the following days, Tawanda and Zech went together into the woods or sat beside the chickee holding hands when no one was looking.

Tobias got stronger and after a long week they finally decided to leave. The Indians had planned a farewell feast for their last night in the village with roasted alligator tail. Zech didn't want to eat it at first, but then he enjoyed the chicken taste of it.

Zech was almost asleep when Tawanda came quietly and lay down next to him. He put his arms around her, enjoying her warmth. She pressed closer, facing him, and they fell asleep. They did not notice Tobias walk past and look at them briefly. Seeing them asleep like children, he turned and walked away.

The next morning Keith told them the best way home. Tobias was still weak but willing to ride. Zech's and Tawanda's eyes met in silent understanding that he would return.

When they were away from the village, Tobias turned to Zech. "I woke up during the night and saw you sleeping with that girl. Did you do anything to her?"

Zech blushed, and said, "No … Pappa … I didn't do anything. We were just asleep together … that's all. We became friends while you were so sick."

Tobias stopped his horse and turned to his son. "I don't have anything against what you did, Zech. I wouldn't mind if you brought an Indian girl home with you for good, and Emma wouldn't either. That's not the point. Just don't ever mess up a girl and then go off and leave her to look after herself. Do you understand what I'm saying?"

"I understand, Pappa. I wouldn't do anything to hurt Tawanda. Not ever!"

Some days later they arrived at their house. Emma ran to them and put her arms around Tobias. "You've been gone so long," she said. "I was worried about you. I'm glad you're back."

Zech said, "Pappa had malaria. That's why we took so long. He was so sick, I thought he would die. An Indian medicine man cured him."

"Tobias!" Emma exclaimed. "You had malaria? Oh Lord! I should have been there with you."

"Don't worry! The Indians looked after me real good. All I need is a few days rest and I'll be fine."

Emma said, "Let's go to the house and I'll fix something to eat. Then I want to hear all about your trip."

SIXTEEN

A cold December wind blew in his face as Zech rode alone across the prairie. He shivered and pulled his jacket tight. Mile after mile of brown prairie all looked the same as he made his way to Fort Drum and the Christmas dance.

The moment he entered the dance hall he was embarrassed. He was dressed in faded jeans, dusty boots and denim jacket, and all the other men and boys wore black suits, white shirts and string ties. Glenda was behind the table serving punch. When she noticed Zech, she waved at him. For a moment he wanted to go back to the prairie where he belonged, but then Glenda came over with a glass of punch.

"I hoped you'd be here tonight," she said. She saw he felt uncomfortable and suggested going outside for some fresh air.

Outside she said, "It's cold! Put your arm around me."

He put his arm around her and told her that he would camp on the prairie over night.

"Zech! You can't do that!" Glenda exclaimed. "It's too cold. You can stay at my house tonight. We have an extra room."

"Your daddy would probably take a whip to me if I even showed up there," Zech said.

"He wouldn't mind at all. I told my mother and father that I love you. So they know about us."

Zech said, "I'd like to stay, Glenda, but it don't seem right."

"It would if we were promised."

"Promised? What's that?"

"You know, going together. Promised to each other. If I'm promised to you, I won't even look at another boy. You can start by kissing me."

He took her in his arms and kissed her, and the smell got to him again.

Finally he relaxed his grip and said. "Don't be mad at me, Glenda, but I can't stay. I got to be home. Pappa needs me to help him with something."

"Well, I guess if you have to, you have to," she said sadly. "But don't you forget we're promised! You hear? I mean it, Zech MacIvey! You're promised to me now!"

On the way back he searched himself for a reason why he lied about having to help his father. He had not hesitated to sleep with Tawanda in his arms, but Glenda's invitation frightened him. He liked Glenda very much, but he could not understand why she had chosen him so quickly over other boys.

No one was in the house but Emma when Zech rode in. When he sat down at the table to eat, she noticed that he was deep in thought. Suddenly Zech said, "Mamma, do you know what it means to be promised?"

"Of course I know. Your father and I were promised. It means you plan to get married someday, and you're not supposed to be with anyone else."

"Can a man like two women at the same time, and like one just as much as the other?"

"I suppose so. But there'll come a time when he has to choose between them. No man can have two wives. It's against the Lord's way."

Zech said, "Mamma, it hurts bad, and I don't know what to do. Me and Glenda got promised last night. But there was a girl in the Indian village. Tawanda ..."

"I knew something happened with you down there. It's up to you. It's your choice, and you'll have to make it. Choose wisely. And don't end up hurting one of them real bad for nothing. Don't make either of them think they're the one if they're not. That wouldn't be fair."

"Thank you for listening, Mamma. I just needed to talk to someone about it."

Emma put her arms around him. "I can see why any girl would want you, Zech. Girls want a man, not some fancy dancer who couldn't skin a rabbit if his family is starving. You don't understand this, but girls do. That's why I chose Tobias."

Zech suddenly realized something he should have known all along: there is more to life than dances or black suits or bowls of punch. He was educated not in reading and writing but in survival, and this was not something he should be ashamed of. His teachers were the best, and he loved them for it. He promised he would never again make excuses to himself or to anyone for what he was or who he was. He was a MacIvey, and proud of it.

He rushed to the door and said, "I think I'll go down in the woods and see if I can shoot a turkey; then I'll cut us a tree. I bought a big bundle of ribbon at the store to decorate it. We've never had a Christmas tree, and it's about time we did."

SEVENTEEN

February
1880

"Emma! Emma! Come and see! They're blooming!" Tobias was running through the woods as fast as his legs would carry him.

Emma hurried from the house. "What on earth is the matter with you, Tobias?"

"The orange trees ...," Tobias shouted. "They are in bloom! Millions of buds. And the smell! You got to see it!"

The shouting had made everybody come out. Pearlie Mae was followed by three little boys she had given birth to.

Three more times Tobias had replanted the orange trees and expanded the plot, and now there were one hundred acres inside a fenced area.

He said to them, "We'll have enough to fill a whole ship at Fort Pierce! That's what the future is – oranges! We don't have to round 'em up or brand 'em, but pick 'em off the trees!"

Emma tried to calm him down as they all followed him through the wood. Row after row of trees seemed to be covered with snow. There was a steady drone as bees were flying from blossom to blossom.

"We should build some beehives," Zech said. "We could get lots of honey out here."

"I could stand here the rest of my life and just sniff," Emma said. "I hope heaven smells like this. But I've got things to do at the house. I'm just getting started with my dress and the wedding is almost here."

Zech and Glenda had finally set their wedding for the last week in February, having honoured her father's request that they wait until she finished four years of school in Jacksonville.

When they were in the house again Zech said to Emma, "Mamma, I'm so glad to see Pappa so happy with the grove. He's worked so hard all these years and finally it's about to pay off. But somebody could come along and take it all away from him, even the house and everything. We don't own this land. I will go to Kissimmee and buy the land. I've found out it's just twenty cents an acre. But don't tell Pappa anything."

"You're doing the right thing, Zech. And don't ever let it bother you that your Pappa doesn't know. Someday he'll be thankful you did this."

"I hope so, Mamma. I don't want to see him hurt; anyone could show up with a deed. That would be the end of it."

Zech came back from the land office smiling, holding the deed in his hands as though it might fly away. The title was in three names, his and Tobias and Emma, and later he would add Glenda's name after she had become a MacIvey.

On his way out of town he bought two suits, white shirts and string ties for himself and Tobias. Then he bought a blue dress for Emma.

Tobias was at the grove and Emma in the house. Zech entered the house, waving the deed, and hugged Emma.

"It's done, Mamma. I bought twenty thousand acres at twenty cents an acre!"

"I'll sleep better knowing that!" said Emma.

"Look here, Mamma, I bought Pappa and I suits for the wedding."

"It'll take a team of oxen to drag him into it," said Emma, laughing.

EIGHTEEN

Zech and Glenda's wedding was a wonderful ceremony. Everybody was dressed in their finest clothes. Zech's heart was pumping wildly as he put the ring on her finger.

However, the MacIveys did not feel very comfortable in their suits and were glad when the ceremony came to an end.

Glenda became a member of the MacIvey clan easily, and Emma liked her immensely, finding in her the daughter she had always wanted. She helped in the kitchen, went into the woods to gather berries and decorated the cabin that Zech had built for them.

One day when Glenda and Emma were talking in the kitchen, Glenda said, "Emma, I've a secret to share. I'm going to have a baby."

"Oh, Glenda, that's wonderful," Emma exclaimed. I'm so happy. Have you told Zech?"

"No, I'm not going for a while yet. I want to go on the drive with all of you. If Zech knew, he wouldn't let me go. I'm only about two months along so he won't notice."

"You are a real MacIvey," Emma said, "as stubborn as Tobias and Zech. But you must promise to turn back if you feel poorly. This baby means more to me than all the gold in Punta Rassa."

"I promise," Glenda answered. "But I know I'll be fine."

NINETEEN

One thousand and eighty cows were on their way to Punta Rassa this time. The men on horseback to the rear followed by Emma, Glenda and Pearlie Mae with her three sons in the ox wagon.

Glenda was fascinated by the wide prairie land. This was her first trip inland and she could not stop looking at the nature and wildlife.

When they finally arrived in Punta Rassa, their herd counted over two thousand. Tobias did not seem to be interested as the sacks of gold coins were placed on the table. Zech took them to the wagon and gave Frog and Skillit their share. He told his mother and Glenda to take what they needed to buy supplies for the return trip and anything else they wanted.

When the two women came back they were dressed in jeans, denim shirts and boots, and Glenda had a black felt hat on.

Frog was the first to notice, and said loudly, "Whoo-ee! Just look at that! They look like drovers now!"

They were five days out of Punta Rassa turning to the northeast toward the lower Kissimmee, when they entered an area of thick palmetto. Glenda and Zech were riding ahead, with Frog and Skillit at the rear, behind the wagon.

The first shot came from the bushes on the right, hitting Glenda's horse in the shoulder. The horse fell forward and Glenda tried to jump from the saddle but the horse crashed down on top of her. Zech turned Ishmael around just as a bullet exploded the horse's brain. He too hit the ground under the horse.

Tobias saw Glenda and Zech struggling to break free; then he pushed Emma from the wagon and jumped on top of her, saving her from more bullets. The horse ran forward, taking the wagon past the dead horses and directly toward the line of fire.

Pearlie Mae jumped from the wagon and ran for a palmetto clump, pulling all three boys with her.

For minutes the men fired their Winchesters. Then they saw two men jumping into the wagon. They struggled with the trunk and pushed it to the rear.

Tobias found the trigger of his shotgun and pulled. There was an overwhelming boom. Both men screamed, as they were knocked backward. One fell down at once. The other tried to stumble away but was hit by a bullet from Frog's Winchester.

Tobias and his men continued shooting until they were sure the danger was over. Then Frog jumped on his horse and galloped full speed into the woods and disappeared.

Emma hurried to Glenda, having seen her go down with the horse, and found her lying in the bushes, feeling her stomach and moaning.

"Emma," she said. "It hurts real bad! I think it's going to come out of me."

Emma turned around and shouted, "Pearlie Mae! Come quick! Bring cloth and water from the wagon! Zech! Come here! Get your tent and put it up here! Hurry!"

Zech came with his tent and said, "They killed Ishmael!"

"Forget the horse!" Emma shouted sharply. "Glenda's hurt! There's no time left! Move quickly!"

As soon as the tent was up, Emma and Pearlie Mae moved Glenda inside. Zech stayed outside but heard Glenda's moans. He ran back and forth until Emma finally came out carrying a small cloth-bound bundle. She went behind the tent and then returned with empty hands.

Zech said, "What's the matter, Mamma? Tell me now! I want to know!"

Emma's eyes filled with tears as she said, "She's had a miscarriage, Zech!"

Zech didn't understand, so Emma continued. "She was pregnant, and she lost the baby. It was a little girl."

"Baby? Glenda was going to have a baby?" Zech's face was first puzzled but then it became red with anger. "I didn't know, Mamma! Why didn't she tell me? I wouldn't have let her come! She had no right to keep this from me!"

"Now don't you start that!" Emma said harshly. "I don't want to hear a word of it! She told me, and I promised not to tell you for the very reason you said! She wanted to come along and be with you and with all of us! She's the bravest girl I've ever known, and you should be proud of her. Now you go in there, and don't say one damned word to make her feel worse than she feels now!"

When he came out of the tent, he turned to Emma and said, "I'm not blaming Glenda now, and I know whose fault it is. It's those bastards out there somewhere. They won't stop till they kill us all, unless I kill them first. And I will."

Suddenly Frog entered the clearing and stopped near Tobias. A man was tied to the horse, a rope around his neck, his hands tied behind him.

"This must be the one whose horse was shot," Frog said. "I found him hiding in a bush."

Tobias said, "Now that you got him, I don't know what to do with him. There ain't no law out here to turn him over to."

"That's for sure," Frog got off his horse. "I should have just shot him out there in the woods."

Zech, who had been watching the scene, dropped his shovel and jumped quickly onto the horse and rode into the woods, pulling the man through the brush. He heard his father shout, "Zech! What the hell are you doing? Come back here!"

He raced full gallop for fifty yards, feeling the body bouncing against the trees; then he stopped and threw the rope over the branch of a tree. There was no fight or cry for mercy as the horse moved forward again, pulling the body upward, dangling it metres up in the air.

When Tobias and the two men reached Zech, Tobias said nothing. He looked into Zech's glazed eyes and knew that any comment would be useless.

"Get him off the tree and bring him to the others and we'll bury them in one grave," he said to Skillit.

One grave was only two feet long, the other huge. Zech had insisted they bury Ishmael too. Crosses made of wood were at the head of each mound.

Zech held Glenda up, his arm tightly around her. Tobias turned to Zech and said, "You want me to say words, or you want to do it yourself?"

"I'll do it myself. It's my baby."

Zech took off the black felt hat and pressed it to his chest. Then the others did the same.

He said, "Lord … bless this little girl … and see to it the wolves don't dig her up. Make her to be a fine woman … like Mamma and Glenda. And Lord … forgive me for what I've done … but the bastard deserved it. Amen."

They gave Glenda some days to get well again, then they put her into the covered wagon, Emma riding with her and Zech driving. Zech glanced at the graves one last time; then he cracked his whip and moved the oxen forward.

TWENTY

September became October, and the men continued to make trip after trip into Fort Pierce, buying barrels to be used when the oranges were picked later that year. It was the end of October when Zech set out alone to buy more marshtackies from the Indians. He found his way with difficulty. When he passed the eastern shore of Lake Okeechobee, something reminded him of Tawanda. Memories that he had pushed away came back.

All of a sudden he was met by an Indian who took him to the village. There he met Keith Tiger who had become an old man. Of course he wanted to know about Tobias and was relieved that he had recovered from his malaria. When he asked why Zech had come, he told him that he needed two marschtackies. Keith Tiger promised to have them in the village the next day.

"It is you, isn't it, Zech?"

When he turned around he was shocked by Tawanda's beauty; the same brown skin and green eyes, the flowing black hair and her athletic body. They talked a little, then rode away from the village and into the forest where they could be alone.

She sat down close to him and put her arms around him, bringing back wonderful memories into his mind.

"Why did you wait so long to come back? I watched the trail each week until finally I gave up. I thought of you all the time, and then I tried to forget you."

"There's something I must tell you, Tawanda," said Zech slowly. "I'm married now."

The words did not shock her. She said, "It doesn't matter. I want to be here with you anyway."

When he told her about Glenda's accident, she was sorry, but after a few moments of silence she said, "We'll spend the night here together. I'll go to the village and get food and blankets. I don't care what my people might think. I'm not promised to any man. I chose not to be."

The night brought back many memories and the two swam in a wave of love. He felt as if he were caught in a hurricane, powerless to control what was happening even if he wanted to.

When they rode into the village together at dawn, Tawanda was smiling and laughing. No protest was made, not even by her father and mother as they watched Zech and Tawanda take food and go off alone. The marshtackies were waiting, and after a final farewell he tied them behind his horse, kissed Tawanda and rode away quickly, not looking back for fear he would return and stay longer.

With each mile he travelled, Zech felt guilty. He tried to push Tawanda from his mind and pretend it had not happened at all, but he knew it had. It was all too real to be make-believe. Finally he made himself believe that what he had done with Tawanda belonged in the swamp and would remain there and had nothing to do with his life with Glenda. These were two separate worlds, one real and one fantasy, and there was no reason for them to ever meet.

TWENTY-ONE

1883/1888

On March 12th, 1883, Glenda gave birth to a healthy baby boy. They called him Solomon MacIvey, and Zech was the proudest father in Florida.

The cattle drives were reduced to one every two years, and much of the grazing was done on MacIvey land. More and more herds were on the prairie and once in a while range wars broke out.

Tobias slowly increased his orange grove to three hundred acres and, besides the cows, the grove alone would provide a good living. However Tobias and Zech realised that keeping cows was in their blood, and they would never be able to give it up.

Zech meanwhile had bought thirty thousand acres of land and planned to look for more land south of Lake Okeechobee, because he felt that his future lay there.

Skillit came home from one of the trips to Kissimmee and he had changed. He tried to avoid the looks of the MacIveys.

Over dinner one evening, he confessed to the family that he had bought some land and wanted to move there with Pearlie Mae and their five children.

Though the family was surprised, Tobias said, "Don't worry. We understand you. And if you need us, we'll come. MacIveys stick together, white or black."

When Skillit's wagon was full of belongings and the oxen he'd bought stood ready to go, the MacIveys hugged and had tears in their eyes. Skillit tried to speak again but he couldn't; he cracked the whip, moved the oxen forward and said, "I got to go now ..."

The others left silently as Tobias and Emma continued watching the wagon until it disappeared into the woods. Tobias said, "It's breaking up, Emma."

"Yes, it is," she said. "But it has to sooner or later. Nothing lasts forever. Everything ends."

She took his hand in hers and they walked slowly back toward the house as if tired.

TWENTY-TWO

1892

"I wish I could make Pappa stay at home," Zech said, eating alone with Glenda. "He'll soon be sixty years old, too old to be out in the prairie."

However, Tobias did not want to stay behind when the other men went on the drive again. Emma had taken good care of him and given him medicine. She made it clear that she was against another drive but knew that her words were in vain.

After they had bought more cows from several small ranchers, they had two thousand of them when they reached Punta Rassa. The market price had gone up to twenty dollars per head, and Zech collected forty thousand dollars in gold coins.

He asked the office person about buying land south of Lake Okeechobee and got the name and address of someone in charge. And as Emma and Glenda were not against him taking the trip, he left the same day.

The owner of the storehouse that also took care of land selling was surprised when he heard that Zech wanted to buy sixty thousand acres and even paid cash. The deed would be ready in two days.

Zech had not thought of Tawanda when he had planned the trip, but now he noticed how close the Seminole village was. On his way there he did not have any expectations. She might be married now with children of her own. Perhaps he would at least be able to speak to her.

He reached the village at noon but found almost all the chickees empty. So he sat down, trying to decide what to do.

Suddenly a marshtackie ridden by a young boy galloped past and disappeared into the woods. Several people then ran into the clearing after the horse.

Tawanda stopped in front of him, staring wide-eyed.

"Zech? Zech? Is it really you? I don't believe it!"

"Yes, Tawanda, it's me," he replied, getting up. "I almost got run over by a horse just now. Who was that boy flying through here on the marshtackie?"

"It was my son, Toby. He rides well, doesn't he?"

"He rides like the wind. You must be real proud of him."

"Yes, I am."

For a moment there was silence. Zech was not sure what to do, scared that an Indian husband might cause trouble if he found them together.

Tawanda broke the silence. "What are you doing here? It's been over nine years, Zech!"

"I had a business at a trading post near by."

They sat down on a bench next to a chickee, Zech moving his fingers nervously against the wood.

"Why are you so nervous, Zech? Is anything wrong?" Tawanda asked.

"Well, yes, it is, Tawanda," he said embarrassed. "Your husband. Where is he now? Will he come here soon?"

"So that's it," she said, smiling. "If that's what's worrying you, you can relax. I have no husband – and Toby – he is your son!"

"Tawanda ... what are you saying? Toby is our son?"

"Yes, we made him that night we spent together in the woods."

Zech was shocked. "Why didn't you send word to me? I would have done something if I had known."

"What would you have done? I need nothing but Toby."

"Damn," he exclaimed. "All this time I've had a son down here and didn't know it! Does he know about me?"

"Yes. Everyone here knows. At first Toby was treated as a half-breed. The boys made fun of him, but no one does now. Many even say that he will become the leader of our people someday. Everyone admires him. You can be proud of him too, Zech."

"Tell me what I can do for him?" Zech asked. "I'll do anything."

"Do for him?" she asked. She thought for a moment, and then she said, "Yes, there is something you can do for him. You can promise me you'll never interfere in his life. Never! You must let him grow up here with his people where he's happy and where he belongs. He will never be part of your world, and you must never tell anyone in your world about Toby. Do you promise, Zech? This is all I ask of you."

"If that is what you want, I promise. But I wish I could do more."

Some minutes later Toby walked over, staring at Zech.

"There's someone here you should know," Tawanda said. "This is your father Zech MacIvey."

Zech tried to smile but couldn't. "Hello, Toby. It's good to know you. You're a fine-looking boy, and you ride as good as anyone I've ever seen."

"You really think so? Would you like to ride the horse?" Toby said, not really knowing what to say.

"Yes, but not now. Let me give you some presents first of all."

Zech walked quickly to his horse and returned carrying the Winchester and a hunting knife. He gave them to Toby and said, "These are for you."

Toby's eyes widened as he turned the rifle over and over in his hands. "You mean this is for me? I can keep the rifle and the knife as my own?"

"They're yours now. And before I leave I'll teach you to shoot the rifle."

Toby was no longer afraid, put the rifle down and ran to Zech, throwing his arms around him, seeking the relation he had always longed for. He said, "Thank you, Father! I've never had such presents!"

"Can I show the rifle and the knife to Billie Bird? He won't believe what I have!"

Tawanda agreed and Toby rushed off, shouting loudly.

That night Zech spread his blanket not far from the beds of Tawanda and Toby. And when Toby was asleep, Tawanda came to him without hesitation. Later they both lay awake, and Zech said to her, "Tawanda … there's something I must say to you, and I hope I say it right. I've loved you since that first time I came here with my pappa, but I love Glenda too. I'll never leave Glenda for you. Mamma told me that I had to choose and I chose Glenda. But it doesn't mean that I wanted you less. You and Toby will always be a part of me."

"I knew you would never be mine," said Tawanda. "I am an Indian and you are white, and these are two worlds that have never come together, and never will. You have given me the one thing I was looking for since the first time you rode into this village … your son."

The next day came all too soon, and Zech knew he could stay no longer. After breakfast he saddled his horse with the feeling that he was leaving a part of himself here and he might never see it again. As he started to mount, Tawanda looked at Toby and said, "Now, Toby."

He boy stepped forward and said, "I thank you again for the gifts … and Father, I love you. Will you come and see me again?"

Zech couldn't hold back his tears. He took Toby in his arms and said, "Yes, Toby … I will. And I love you too. Very much. There is one thing I ask of you … Please take care of your mother for me. Will you do this, Toby?"

"I will look after her as you would, if you were here with us."

He could take no more of it. He looked deep into Tawanda's eyes; then he mounted his horse and rode away quickly.

As he made his way to the trading post, one thing became clear to him. He knew now that fate had given him two lives, two families, and he accepted it without question. He reached the trading post and took the deed, but set off at once because he wanted to be home as soon as possible.

When he rode into the clearing Glenda came to him. He jumped off the horse and took her in his arms, kissed her and said, "I love you, Glenda. I really do … and I want you to know it."

"Did you get what you wanted?" she asked.

"Yes, I did. And even more than I expected," said Zech, then realized that he had almost said too much and added, "even more land than I thought."

TWENTY-THREE

It was just past noon as the MacIvey caravan crossed Kissimmee River. Although Tobias had become stronger, they stopped early each day on the return trip to give him some rest.

Everyone but Tobias and Emma rode away to hunt deer or turkey for the evening meal.

Emma prepared the meal. One of her greatest satisfactions was cooking the meals and the joy everyone had eating them. She decided to go into the woods and pick some berries for a special pie. Deeper and deeper she went and almost lost time in the beauty of nature.

Suddenly pain hit her, causing her to stumble and fall to the ground. She tried to get up but couldn't, then it came again, a flash that burned into her chest like a branding iron.

Sweat poured from her face. For several minutes she lay on her back, unable to sit up. She was afraid of dying alone in the wood, without Tobias around her. With this thought she tried to get to her feet and slowly she managed to reach the clearing where Tobias saw her at once.

"Emma! ... Emma! ... What in the name of God is wrong with you?"

She said feebly, "The pain, Tobias ... it hurts so bad. It came on me sudden ..." Then she stumbled and fell to the ground.

Tobias dropped down next to her and wiped the sweat from her forehead.

"Oh God! ... Emma ... Don't you leave me, Emma ... You hear me! ... Don't you leave ..."

She looked at him, her eyes were clear; then her hand went to his. She said, "Tobias … Tobias. I'm sorry …" Then the last flicker of life went out of her.

Tobias shook her gently and then violently, shouting her name with pain.

Zech came on his horse, saw his mother and father and jumped off the horse next to them. He stared at them but could not believe what he saw.

Slowly Tobias said, "Zech, she is gone from us. And it ain't fair."

They wrapped Emma's body in a blanket, and Frog and Bonzo were sent home to prepare a coffin.

They reached the hammock the following evening. Glenda and Zech dressed Emma in the blue dress she had worn to their wedding and laid her in the coffin in the kitchen.

Tobias refused to move when everybody went to bed. Zech could not sleep so he got up again and joined his father.

Tobias turned to him and said, "You know, Zech. It was your mamma who held the family together when times were roughest. And I never did nothin' for her. With all the gold in the trunks I could've bought her fancy dresses and shoes and such as a woman likes, but all I ever gave her was that goddam cook stove. And now it's too late to do anything. I waited too long."

It worried Zech that his father felt this way about Emma, so he said, "She didn't want stuff like that, Pappa. All she wanted was to be with us, and you made her as happy as she could be. She told me that several times. She loved you, Pappa. More than anything."

"She told you this?" Tobias asked. "You really heard her say that?"

"Many times, Pappa. Me and her used to talk a lot before I got married."

Tobias thanked Zech for his kind words. "I'll rest after Emma is at peace in her own ground," he said quietly. "This is the last night I'll ever get to spend with Emma in the house and I want to make the most of it."

The hole had been dug in the morning. Zech, Frog and Bonzo carried the coffin with Tobias, Glenda and Sol following. When it had been lowered into the earth, Tobias stepped to the foot of the grave, bowed his head in silence, and then said in broken words, "The Good Book says the Lord has given ... and the Lord has taken back ... but this time, Lord, You took back an awful lot. There ain't never been no finer woman put on earth than Emma. I thank You for the time we spent together ... and I wish You had let her stay with me longer. I'll miss her powerfully ... and I don't understand why she had to go instead of me. I don't think it's fair, but that's Your judgement ... but take her to You with the same love she had when she was here. Amen."

Tobias threw in the first shovel of dirt. Then he stood by and watched as the grave filled. He was still standing there when Zech came back an hour later with a large bunch of wild flowers.

TWENTY-FOUR

1894

For over a year, Tobias was in pain, seldom leaving the clearing and with no interest for cows or anything else. After this period of time he turned his attention back to the orange grove, his one personal pride and satisfaction, and he spent most of his time there, often just sitting alone among the trees. But his health was becoming weaker and weaker.

Glenda took over all of the chores that Emma had done, never complaining or asking for help.

Zech and the men started fencing the MacIvey land, but the fences were often cut. The fence was built to keep the herd together on their own land instead of driving them over the prairie. Zech was angry when he saw that there was a lot of stealing of cows. He thought he knew where the rustlers came from. Tawanda had told him about a man called Wirt McGraw and a group of dangerous men living on the ten thousand islands. But he was not ready to take action yet.

It was late December when it started to freeze. Tobias had tried to pick as many oranges as possible. With a strong wind came freezing temperatures. The temperature dropped to fourteen degrees and kept the family inside. Tobias watched the thermometer with fear. He often went out into the grove to check the trees and the oranges.

One day he came into the room, poured himself a mug of coffee and said, "Fourteen degrees. That means the oranges are gone. And if it holds for much longer, the trees'll go too."

Two days later the weather changed. A clear sky and brilliant sun woke them up in the morning, and the temperature rose quickly to seventy-five degrees. The oranges were frozen and most of the leaves were dead but the trees would survive if it stayed warm.

A month later Tobias came running into the house and reported that the trees were showing the first blossoms again.

In February Zech noticed, standing in the garden, that the sky was becoming darker and darker, and thunder could be heard in the distance. Rain came steadily in the afternoon but shortly after dark the wind got up and the temperature dropped quickly.

Tobias ran through the kitchen unsteadily. "I don't like the feel of this," he said to Zech. "It's more than a rainstorm for sure."

"You're just too negative, Pappa," Zech answered. "There's just no way we're going to have another storm like that last one."

But the wind grew stronger and even the temperature in the house dropped.

Tobias dressed and rushed outside, and what he saw surprised him. Eleven degrees, and what had been rain was now sleet. Every tree was ice-covered, and the ground was one solid sheet of ice. At midnight, snow came, a blizzard turned everything into a sea of white.

The men constantly had to see to the fire around which everybody had gathered. Just before nightfall Zech, Frog and Bonzo went into the yard and brought more wood. Meanwhile they had to go into the wood and gather broken branches that could not carry the weight of the snow. Tobias insisted on helping.

It was when Glenda put supper on the table that Tobias' absence was noticed. All of them had thought that he had gone to his bedroom, but it was empty.

Zech went out into the darkness to find his father. When he finally reached the outside edge of the grove, he saw a fire glowing. Tobias was standing there, trying to warm himself, his frozen beard covered with ice.

Zech ran towards him and shouted harshly, "Pappa! What the hell you mean coming out here? It'll be the death of you!"

Tobias turned to him and said calmly, "I had to come here, Zech. I've got to save at least one tree, and the heat of this fire is the only way. There won't be nothin' left to take cuttings from and start the grove again. I've got to save one tree!"

"Damn them trees, Pappa! After this is over we can grow another tree somehow, but we can't grow another you!"

Finally Zech grabbed him. He tried to struggle free but he was too feeble. Zech took him to the house and sat him next to the fireplace.

Tobias was in bed and Zech sat at his side.

"You got to promise me something, Zech," Tobias said. "You'll replant the trees. Oranges is the best way to go. Better than cows. Don't have to chase 'em. You got to promise."

"I promise, Pappa. Just get some rest. We'll talk about it later."

Then he fainted again.

Just before noon Tobias woke up again. He looked at Zech and smiled, and then he said, "Did you keep the fire going?"

"Never mind the fire, Pappa. Just keep still and you'll feel better."

"I ain't going to be fine, Zech … and I know it … and I'm not afraid. I'm done with it now. And you know something, Zech … Glenda is a fine woman and a fine cook and I truly thank her for all she's done for us … but I ain't had a biscuit like Emma's since she left us … Maybe Emma's got a cook stove up there with her."

Tears came into Zech's eyes when Tobias continued, "We did some great things, didn't we, Zech?"

"Yes, Pappa, we sure did do some great things. We surely did."

"We done … some things … Zech … you and me …" Zech became quiet as his father lay still.

"Oh, Pappa," he cried. "Why'd you have to die? Damn trees!"

Zech sat on the edge of the bed for several minutes, feeling that a part of him had died also.

The next morning the sleet stopped but the earth was still frozen and covered with ice. Zech went into the woods to find some signs of life, but all animals were dead or gone, and it was an unknown silence that was everywhere.

When he came in again, he sat down with Glenda at the table and said, "It's down to just you and me and Sol now, and from what I've seen out there so far, we're back to where this family was twenty-five years ago. I hope there's a few rabbits and raccoons still alive, 'cause it might be all that's left to eat. It's going to be a long time before we get over this."

"We'll make it, Zech. We'll do whatever we have to do."

"You know something else," he said, reaching out and touching her hand. "All that gold we got can't be stewed or fried. It's not worth a damn unless I can find supplies. But everybody out there will be doing the same."

"You should go to Fort Drum. Pappa will let us have whatever he can give," Glenda said.

Then he stood up and said, "That's a good idea, and I'll do it. But first I'm going to gather some of the frozen animals. Maybe we can smoke 'em."

When the ice had finally melted, they dug a grave for Tobias. Frog had told Skillit the news about Tobias' death and now they were all standing at the open grave.

After lowering the coffin Zech stepped forward to say a few last words. He spoke slowly, "Lord, bless Pappa ... and see to it he's with Mamma again, where he wants to be. Pappa was a good man, Lord. I've never known him to do a bad thing ... not ever. Lord ... one more thing ... please don't throw nothing more like this at me any time soon ... I don't think I can stand it. Amen."

TWENTY-FIVE

The whole area was devastated. Only buzzards were alive feeding themselves with the dead animals lying everywhere. At least Zech had managed to buy some flour to help them through the rest of the winter. He had also learned that there was one place deep in the south east, Fort Dallas, which the freeze had not visited, and he planned to buy orange trees there to rebuild the groves.

It was six weeks after the freeze when Zech saw a caravan of people coming closer from the south. He was surprised when he finally noticed that they were Indians and when the leading Indian had reached him it was Keith Tiger who talked to him.

"It is good to see you again, Zech MacIvey," said Keith. "You look more like your father each time we meet." Zech looked at the thirty people in front of him but saw that Tawanda was not with them, only her father, Tony Cypress, was there.

"We've come to pay our last respects to Tobias," said Keith Tiger.

Zech was overwhelmed. "You've come all this way to do this? Pappa would be real pleased."

He led them to the grave. There, Keith asked him to leave them alone so they could hold an Indian ceremony. On his way back to the house Zech heard them singing mournfully.

A while later he rode back to the Indians to invite them for supper. They refused his offer and wanted to stay in their tents that they had put up. When Zech offered them presents, they gladly accepted several cases of bullets that Zech fetched from the house.

The next time Zech saw Tony Cypress, he asked about Tawanda. He was shocked to hear that she was dead. She had died in childbirth. Tears came into his eyes especially when it became clear that he had been the father of the baby.

"Then it's my fault!" he said. "I killed her."

"Do not feel this way," Tony Cypress said. "I don't hold you responsible. You made her happy, and we thank you for this. Tawanda died happy. We believe that one who dies in sadness can never rest easy in the afterlife."

Tobias felt a little relieved. "I thank you for what you're saying. If you felt otherwise, I don't know what I'd do. You should know I loved Tawanda, and I told her so."

"We know this. We are proud that MacIvey blood flows in Toby. He has never forgotten your last visit and speaks of you with much pride." Then he added, "You have no reasons for guilt in your words. Remove this from your heart and replace it with happy memories. Will you do this for me and Tawanda?"

"I'll try to remember only the good," answered Zech, and when he mounted his horse to ride away, he thought of the two days he had spent with Tawanda and Toby, and the light of the joy he had seen in Tawanda's face.

TWENTY-SIX

While nature recovered slowly, the men of the MacIvey hammock spent two months preparing the orange grove for new trees.

Zech put Frog in charge of the homestead and he, Sol and Glenda set out on the journey to Fort Drum in order to buy new orange trees. Their first half of the trip took them easily to Palm Beach within five days.

When they came to Palm Beach, it was like entering a fantasy world for Zech, Glenda and Sol. Stores along the main street were selling fashion from Paris and London, fine wines, sausages and cheese from New York.

Suddenly they saw it, the Royal Poinciana Hotel, one of the largest wooden buildings in the world and, with 1,150 guest rooms, the largest hotel anywhere.

Twelve hundred windows blinked back at Zech, who stared at the building with his open mouth and exclaimed, "God a'mighty, just look at that! I didn't know that there were enough trees in all the world to make that many boards to build it."

"Let's stay in it tonight, Pappa!" Sol said excitedly.

They decided to find out the price and at least to have a look inside.

When they saw the elegant interior, Sol was fascinated by the light that was different from what he knew.

"They're electric lights," Zech explained. "I heard about them in Fort Pierce. A fellow named Ed-son made it, and also made a thing that makes music come out of a box."

Zech tried to get a room but was told by a man in a white suit that they needed reservations. Anyway, they were astonished at the price of three hundred dollars for a suite and realized that they were not very welcome.

Sol came back from looking at the side rooms. "Pappa, you should see that room over there! It's an indoor outhouse and when you pull a chain, it washes everything away with water!"

They finally went back to the main street and walked the sidewalks, looking into the storefronts with fascination. In the evening they found a boarding house and enjoyed a huge portion of fried chicken.

The next day they took off to Fort Dallas and discovered that the journey there would be no pleasure trip. They had to ride through swarms of mosquitoes for miles and miles. The further south they moved, the worse the trail became and three days later they reached some kind of jungle.

"It seems like the end of the world," said Glenda. "And I can't for the life of me see why anyone would ever want to live here."

"There'll be people enough when they find out it didn't freeze here," replied Zech.

Then the small trail through the bushes opened and they could see Fort Dallas. They managed to find a shop where they could buy orange trees. Zech bought a full load and made a deal with the owner to get another thousand more shipped in by a ship to Fort Pierce each month.

Glenda had agreed to Zech's idea of buying land with the rest of the money. So Zech bought six thousand acres of land and for Sol he bought a small island called Key

Biscayne that they could see in front of the lagoon. The land seller told them the village that would be built right where they were standing would be called Miami, an Indian name for "very large".

"Maybe someday we could build a little cabin here like the one in Punta Rassa. We could come down by boat from Fort Pierce. It might be fun to come back once in a while and eat fish and mangoes."

"Let's do it!" Sol exclaimed. "Next time we're here I want to see my island. I want to see what's over there, Pappa."

TWENTY-SEVEN

Spring
1896

Zech stood at an empty holding pen, which was some miles south of the hammock.

"A hundred cows!" Zech exclaimed. "Damn! If this keeps up, we might as well let these thieves drive the whole herd to Punta Rassa and sell it themselves."

Frog rode to him, saying, "I've found where they camped, Mister Zech. There are empty cans of beans in the forest. They were there maybe two days ago."

Rustling had become a regular crime against cattle ranchers. The rustlers slaughtered the cows and sold the meat. So no one knew who the owner was.

Zech had sometimes thought about following those men but the tracks told them there were probably about 16 of them. Too many for Zech and his two men. But Frog noticed that this time Zech looked angrier than usual.

After supper, during which Zech had not talked at all, he said to Frog. "What is the roughest town you know, Frog, with the meanest men? We need some gunslingers, can you get me some?"

"Of course I know a place like that. It's Arcadia. How many guys should I get? For just a shot of liquor each, you could get the most fearsome fellows you ever saw."

Glenda was shocked but she saw that she would not be able to stop Zech's plans.

"I want six men," Zech said. "I'll pay five hundred each for the job. We'll get these men who are thieving our cows."

"But how do you know where the rustlers are? They could be anywhere," Frog said.

"Indians once told me that a rustler named Wirt McGraw lives in a camp with a big gang of rustlers in the area of the ten thousand islands," said Zech. "We'll find them easily."

When he asked Frog and Bonzo, only Frog wanted to join them. So Bonzo was told to stay behind and take care of the hammock.

Word of Zech's mission had spread around the surrounding area, and seven local cowmen said they would ride with him. Glenda and Sol wanted to join the group as well but Zech did not allow them to risk their lives. He let them follow the group as far as Punta Rassa and no further.

They decided that Frog would meet them there with the six gunmen he'd found in Arcadia.

The group arrived in Punta Rassa. But when Zech saw Frog's gunmen, even he was frightened. He said to Frog, "God a'mighty. That's the meanest looking bunch I've ever seen."

The men left in the morning. Glenda looked at the group from the porch. Ten minutes later she suddenly heard a horse galloping past the front of the cabin. She rushed outside to see Sol riding after the men.

"Sol! Sol MacIvey!" she shouted. "Come back here!" But Sol did not hear his mother; he rode on into the woods ahead of him.

Late in the afternoon they reached the area where Zech supposed the rustlers to be. The men rode silently, and when night came they stopped and made camp without a fire.

In the morning they set out again, riding slowly towards the rustlers' camp. Finally they dismounted and crept forward, hiding behind some bushes.

They saw several cabins and some fireplaces. On one of them, a cow was roasting. Zech counted twenty-three men who must have felt so safe that they didn't even have guards around the camp.

Zech said, "They are no more of them than there are of us. We'll catch them by surprise. We'll divide our men into three groups. Frog, you take your men around to the south. Six of you stay here with me, and the rest can come in from the east."

Zech knew that someone would have to die, maybe them and maybe himself. "Is it really worth all this?" he asked himself. "All of this possible death just for cows?" But he knew it was more than cows that brought him here. He remembered the dogs and the horses and the bushwhacking and the murder of an unborn baby. He had to stop it. He had to kill these men.

With a shout to the other men he raced his horse forward. They were within one hundred yards of the camp before they were noticed. The rustlers scrambled away but Zech aimed his Winchester and shot the nearest men.

The three attacking groups had the surprised men in a trap. Nine men lay dead already and three more were hurt and crawling in the dirt. The others threw down their rifles and held their arms upward. Frog had been hit in the shoulder but no more of Zech's men were hurt.

He shouted, "Which one of you varmints is Wirt McGraw, the boss of your group?"

A man with a wooden leg came forward. He was old and ugly and he said sharply, "I am, if it's any of your damned business! And who are you?"

"Zech MacIvey."

"MacIvey, eh. I'll remember the name. When you fools are done with whatever you're here for, I'll take care of you, MacIvey. You can count on it."

"Only thing you can count on is the fires of hell!" Zech shot back. "We're goin' to hang the whole lot of you!"

None of them noticed the black marshtackie as it came across the cane field and stopped at the edge of the clearing. The blast of a rifle caught them by surprise, and they turned to see what had happened. A man staggered from the corner of a hut, a hole in his forehead. He fell, firing his rifle as he went down. The bullet hit Zech's right foot like a hammer, knocking him out of his saddle.

Zech jumped up quickly and saw Sol's horse walk forward, the Winchester smoking. Sol shouted, "I had to shoot him, Pappa! He was aiming at you! I had to do it!"

"What the hell are you doing here?" Zech demanded. "I told you to stay in Punta Rassa!"

"I wanted to come, Pappa. I wanted to be here with you!"

"Well, what's done is done. And if you hadn't been here, that bastard would have blown off my head! I thank you for that, Sol!"

When they had everyone tied with ropes, MacGraw spoke, "You fellows wouldn't do something like that to an old army soldier, would you? I lost my leg fightin' for the Rebs in the war."

"That ain't what they say in Punta Rassa," Zech said. "They told me you were a damn deserter who stole from every home you could find."

When finally they mounted the horses, men were hanging from the branches of the trees around the camp.

Back at home Zech lay on a bed as the doctor examined his foot. The doctor shook his head. "I've never seen one like this before. The bullet got stuck in the bone. There is no way I can get it out. I just don't have the tools to do it. The only thing I can do is to take off the foot part way up your leg."

"Hell fire no!" Zech roared. "You ain't goin' to cut off my leg!"

"The nearest places with bone specialists are Jacksonville and Atlanta," said the doctor. "They're miles away."

"There's no way I can stand this much longer. I'd never make it to those doctors," said Zech. For a moment he thought hard, and then he said, "I know what I'll do. I'll go to the same doctor that helped Pappa once. The Seminole medicine man!"

The doctor was furious and said it was a stupid idea, but Zech and Sol packed some food and left immediately.

There were times on their journey when Zech didn't know who or where he was, the pain that shot up his leg like boiling fire was so bad. They reached the Okeechobee trading post at dawn the next day and two hours later they came into the village.

Zech almost fainted in his saddle as Keith Tiger came to him. "Zech? Zech MacIvey? What's wrong? You seem to be in much pain."

"My foot." Zech muttered. "Bullet. Medicine man."

Toby Cypress then came scrambling from a chickee and said, "Father! It is you! What is the matter?"

Sol watched Tiger and the strange boy help Zech from the horse and carry him gently to a table, the words "father ... it is you" ringing in his ears. Then he jumped from the horse and helped them.

The medicine man was now very old. He took the foot in his hand and stared at it. Then he drew a long hunting knife from his belt and pushed the blade into a fire.

Three men came to the table and held Zech down. Miami Billie said, "This will hurt you, but it will soon be over. Put this stick in your mouth and bite it."

Zech bit the stick as the medicine man pulled out the bullet with the knife and his teeth. When he had torn it out he spat it onto the table and said, "I will bandage it now. You may limp, MacIvey, but you will walk."

Those were the last words Zech heard before he fainted, "... you will walk."

When Zech woke up an hour later, Sol and Toby were standing by the table. Sol was both puzzled and hostile as he stared at Toby and then looked at his father. Zech knew why. "You heard what Toby said, didn't you?"

"I heard him call you "father". What does this mean, Pappa? Do Indians call everybody that?"

"No, they don't. Toby is my son, Sol, and your half-brother. His mamma was Tawanda. She's dead now. I promised that you and Glenda would never know about this, but what's done can't be helped. You got to promise me you'll never tell your mamma, Sol. Promise me now!"

"All right, Pappa, I promise. I won't ever tell."

"I knew Tawanda before I married your mamma, and I ain't done anything like that with anyone else ... Now go and do something together. Hunt or fish or ride horses. Get to know each other while you got the chance."

The boys looked at each other.

"I bet my marshtackie is faster than yours," said Sol.

"We'll see," Toby responded, and they both rushed to their horses.

Zech stayed in the village for six more days. The boys spent every day together, racing on horses and fishing. On the morning of the seventh day, Sol and Toby said warm good-byes, promising to see each other again someday. Then Zech and Sol mounted their horses and with a final farewell they left the village.

TWENTY-EIGHT

March
1898

"Mister Zech, how we gone ever put a mark on that big mother?" Frog asked, looking into the pen.

Inside the pen was a Brahma bull, fifteen hundred pounds of anger against the men who put him there. Zech had bought him from a Texan who had brought six of them to Kissimmee by rail.

"He's ugly," said Glenda. "Mean and ugly."

Zech was sure that this bull would start a new era in his business. People wanted more and better meat, and the bull could breed with his cows to produce bigger, stronger calves.

"We'll leave him until tomorrow. He will get calmer," said Zech and rode off with Glenda.

That night they enjoyed some time to themselves. Glenda suggested taking a train down to Fort Drum the next week and building a cabin, just for the two of them, where they could eat fresh fish and mangoes and grow old together.

The next morning they all rode to the pen again. The bull had not quietened down yet.

Frog said, "Me and Bonzo'll go in there and try to get him on the ground. I'd like to be the one to stick a hot iron to him."

"Be careful," Zech warned him.

Frog and Bonzo eased through the gate, and the bull turned to face them immediately. Frog threw a rope around the neck. Suddenly, hell broke loose. The bull wanted to break free, dragging the struggling Frog in the dirt.

Zech shouted, "Frog! Let go and get the hell out of there!"

Frog didn't let go. The bull saw his prey. One horn smashed through Frog's rib cage and sent him hurling eight feet backward.

Zech saw the bull rush past him and right into Glenda's horse. She fell to the ground. Zech could only watch horrified as the horns rammed into Glenda, going into her stomach and ripping upward.

He heard her scream, "Zech! Help me!"

The first bullet caused the bull to stagger, the second brought it down. As it hit the ground Glenda came loose and tumbled away. Zech ran as fast as he could. He snatched the smoking rifle away from Sol and fired into the dead animal again and again until the chamber was empty, then fell beside Glenda.

Blood came from her mouth and from her open stomach as she tried to speak. She gurgled, and then silence came and her head rolled to the side.

"Oh no ...," Zech moaned. "Oh no ... Glenda ..."

He fell across her body, soaking himself with blood.

"Mister Zech!" Bonzo shouted from behind. "Frog's hurt real bad! What you want me to do?"

He finally turned around and said, "Hurry! Bring blankets from the house."

Sol staggered forward, his face white and his legs trembling. Then he said, "Is she dead, Pappa? Is Mamma dead?"

"She's gone from us, Sol." He held Glenda in his arms until Bonzo came back.

When they reached the hammock, Zech and Bonzo put Frog on his bunk, wrapped in cloth to stop the bleeding; then Zech carried Glenda into the house alone. He came back out and said to Bonzo, "Go down to the barn and start a coffin. And while you're at it, you might as well make two."

When Bonzo had left, Zech sat on the stoop, his face buried in his hands, remembering, thinking of things done and not done, said and not said.

He looked up and saw Sol sitting next to him.

"Sol," he said. "Don't ever get yourself tied up with a woman, it's like owning dogs. You get to liking them, and it hurts powerful when they go away. I don't know what I'm going to do without your mamma. I don't know if I can make it or not, or even if I want to try."

"We'll be fine, Pappa," Sol said, putting his arm around Zech's shoulder. "Mamma would want us to try, and you know that."

When Zech left Glenda's body, he went to Frog and sat beside his bunk. Frog smiled when he woke up and saw Zech. "Mister Zech, I want to ask you for a favor."

"Sure, Frog. Anything you say."

"I came here to help on one cattle drive, and I stayed here. This hammock's my home. I'd like to be buried right next to Mister Tobias and Miss Emma. Don't put me way off in the woods by myself, Mister Zech."

"You'll rest right next to Mamma and Pappa, but I would have done that even if you hadn't asked."

"That's not all of it, Mister Zech. I got a good bit of gold. I want you to get me a headstone with it. And I'd like the stone to say Frog MacIvey."

Zech reached down and touched his hand. "You are family, and I'll be right proud to get the stone just the way you want it."

"Thank you, Mister Zech," Frog said, smiling again. "I'll tell Mister Tobias you done a good job here after he left, and about all them trees you planted. He'll be right pleased."

His eyes closed, and minutes later he was dead.

Zech and Bonzo dug the holes for the coffins. Then they were lowered into the ground. The three of them stood there silently for a while until Zech finally said, "Lord … I'm not going to say much about this, because I'm sure I can't stand it. I want you to forgive me for buyin' that damned bull, 'cause all I done it for was to make money, and I'll never do nothin' like that again. So help me, Lord, I promise it, but it's too late now for Glenda and Frog. They suffered because of what I've done. Lord bless Glenda. She was as fine a woman as You ever made, and I loved her truly. And bless Frog too. Make them a home with Mamma and Pappa … and see to it they're happy now … Amen."

Zech then turned to Sol. "I'm going to go now, son, to Fort Drum, to see Glenda's parents. When you and Bonzo get done covering the graves, I want you to get all the flowers you can find in the woods and put them on your mamma's grave. She liked pretty things, and she'd appreciate that. And I would too."

TWENTY-NINE

Summer
1905

The drive in the summer of 1898 had been the last for MacIvey cattle, and it was the one that set Zech on a new course, concentrating on smaller numbers of quality meat. He had bought a new sort of bull that changed the herd a lot. All shipments to market were now made by rail, and the old trails leading to Punta Rassa were a thing of the past.

Meanwhile the war against Cuba had broken out and the soldiers who were stationed outside Tampa meant good customers and high prices for the cattle.

Zech had fenced twenty thousand acres of land and had hired gunmen to protect his property.

He made four trips to Okeechobee to see Toby and also to buy the land where the forest that his father had liked so much was. He bought it because he wanted to leave it in its natural state and be sure that no one ever put axes or machines to it.

All of the improvements he made to the orange grove and the cattle operation he made for Sol, not for himself. After Glenda's death he had no use for money or any desire for anything except to build something better for Sol. Money that they earned still went into trunks stored in the old house.

The next day brought lots more rain. Black clouds boiled angrily overhead. Zech had just taken the new bull into the barn. Then Zech mounted his horse and rode away into the rain that poured into his face.

He soon came to the creek and gazed across it, seeing that the level had risen two feet. Suddenly the horse slid and then stumbled as it went down the muddy bank, plunging into the water and Zech was thrown from the saddle. Both horse and rider went under and then came up a few yards downstream.

Zech thought he had come free, but then he felt a tugging as the horse swam desperately against the current. He knew now that his lame foot was caught in the stirrup, pulling him under water. He held his breath as he went under, trying to free the foot, feeling water rush over him, holding his breath until his lungs could stand it no longer. He screamed for mercy; then he let go and sucked for air, pulling a flood of brown water inside him.

Faces and images rushed through his mind, Tobias and Emma and Glenda and Tawanda and Toby and Skillit; Ishmael tied to the garden fence; Nip and Pip rushing after cows; Frog eating ten biscuits and asking for more. And then he was free, free of the pain in his leg, free of the struggling horse and the rushing water. Sol came to him and his last conscious thought was, "Don't grieve, Sol … Don't ever grieve …"

Sol was standing on the stoop worried because Zech had not yet returned. Then he saw the horse, moving slowly into the clearing toward the barn. He saw a form being dragged through the mud, the body of a man.

Sol jumped from the stoop screaming, "Pappa! Pappa! Why did you have to die?!"

He could not get the foot free, so he ran into the house and returned with a knife, cutting the stirrup from the saddle and then carrying Zech's lifeless body inside.

THIRTY

1908

Sol was sitting at the kitchen table studying a pile of papers. He was about to leave the hammock and make the Lardys responsible for the house. Jessie and Tim Lardy had been the MacIvey's cook and housekeeper for the past eight years. He had also hired a man named Ron Clayton, his wife and three young boys to come and live on the place. Clayton would take over as manager of the orange grove and cattle operations and be paid a monthly salary plus a percentage of the yearly profits. He had been told that Bonzo and the Lardys had the right to live on the hammock.

When he had stored all the papers in the room with the trunks he left waving good-bye, promising to visit as often as possible. Then he rode to the graves of his family and stood at the five stones for a while. Thoughts about the past rushed through his mind and tears came into his eyes.

"Goodbye, all of you. I'm sorry to leave but I've got to do it."

Then he got onto the wagon and turned it west toward Punta Rassa.

THIRTY-ONE

South Okeechobee

1911

The two areas of land Zech had bought south of Lake Okeechobee were right in the middle of what was to become the most extensive farmland in South Florida.

Sol noticed that for the last years there were more and more canals, carrying away the water before men turned the wild vegetation into farmland.

Sol learned from the other farmers and started the same process with his land. He started the MacIvey Produce Company and hired workers to plant tomatoes and beans and squash and celery and corn and cucumbers and lettuce, and had become a supplier of vegetables to the growing cities of South and Mid Florida and even Chicago, New York and Boston.

One day, when Sol inspected his farmland south of the lake, he decided to ride down to the Indian village to find out about Toby and his family.

When he reached the village, it was still as he remembered from his last visit seven years before. Toby saw him and shouted, "Sol! How long have you been here? It's good to see you again after such a long time."

For a long time they talked about what had happened in their different worlds. Finally they came to the reason why Sol was in the area.

"You know, I've been very busy. Pappa owned two sections of land below the lake, and I've been clearing them for farming. We're working up north of here now."

Toby's eyes flashed in surprise. He said, "You mean it is you who is destroying the land? I cannot believe this. Father would have never put an axe to the trees. He loved them. Why are you doing this?"

Sol was shocked by Toby's reaction. "Like I said, Toby, I'm turning it into farmland. People in the new cities have to eat, and there's more and more of them. I'm growing vegetables in the fields."

"Animals have to eat too, and so do birds, and so do we!" Toby said angrily. "Will your machines not stop until they come here and crush my mother's grave? I hope they never enter this swamp. If they do, you will have destroyed us too, all of us!"

Sol wished he had never mentioned his work. He said, "It's just swamp, Toby. And there's much more of it."

"It is not just swamp!" Toby replied harshly. "It is God you are killing. He put the land here for all creatures to enjoy, and you are destroying it. When you destroy the land, you destroy God. Go now and stand in the middle of your fields. Count the deer you see, and the alligators, and the fish, and the birds. Count them, Sol, and then tell me how many are still there. You have crushed them with your damned machines."

Sol got up and said, "I'm sorry you feel this way, Toby. But it's my land now, and I have the right to do whatever I want with it."

"You are a traitor to the wishes of your father!" Toby said. "He told me himself he bought the forest so no one could ever put an axe to it, and you have cut it all down! He would die a second death if he knew this!"

Sol mounted his horse and said, "I've done what I thought was right, but no matter what a person does, he can't please everybody. I'm sorry." Then he rode away without looking back.

He felt sick on the way back, the word "traitor" still ringing in his ears. He said to himself that Toby would soon forget this, and they would become friends again. And what little land he had cleared would not make that much difference anyway. There was still a lot of land left, more than anyone could ever use.

It was Saturday, and the farm workers had left for the weekend. Sol felt lonely. There was nothing to do in the villages. So he decided to take one of his Ford T trucks and went to West Palm Beach.

He stopped in front of the Royal Poinciana Hotel. The doorman came down and looked at him and his truck with hostility and shouted, "Get that damned thing out of here!"

"I'm a customer," he said. "And you better let the truck sit right here till I come back or I'll put your little hat right up your ass!" And he walked straight into the lobby.

When he wanted to get a room, it was exactly the same as years before. No rooms were vacant and he needed reservations anyway. Before he left Sol said angrily, "My name is MacIvey. Sol MacIvey. I want you to remember this. You folks pulled that reservation shit on my pappa when mamma wanted to stay here. One of these days I'll build my own hotel, and it'll be much better than this dump. So damn you and your stinkin' rooms!"

When he got back to the truck, he drove it off the driveway and right down the middle of a flowerbed, hearing the doorman run after him, screaming.

An hour later, Zech went into a café. A waitress came over and handed Sol a menu. She was about twenty, with long blonde hair and blue eyes. Her figure filled the uniform to perfection.

Sol found he was shy and didn't know how to speak to her. "What's your name?" he stuttered, when she came to take his order.

"Call me Bonnie," she smiled, showing perfect white teeth. "Now what'll you have to eat?"

Sol ordered a beer and a meal and made some small talk with her. As she was afraid of getting into trouble with her boss, they made a date after her shift later that day.

When they met at five o'clock in a bar around the corner, Sol suggested that she worked for him. "I need someone to do the cooking and look after the house. I'll pay you a hundred dollars a month."

She was happy to get such a well-paid-job and quickly accepted his offer. They decided not to go back to her home to get her clothes because she was afraid of her father, but to buy new ones in the stores instead.

When they were sitting in the truck leaving Palm Beach, she said, "I don't believe this! I thought I would never get out of that café. And you step right in, a real nice fellow, good-looking. I guess I'm about the luckiest girl in West Palm Beach. I'm sure glad you stopped at the café."

THIRTY-TWO

1918

The Ford car drove fast along the road past the lake.

"That letter has really upset you, hasn't it?" asked Bonnie.

"Tim Lardy would never have written me to come back in a hurry unless something is very wrong."

Bonnie and Sol lived together. She was a housekeeper, but she was also a friend, a lover, and a business partner. She did all the office work and her advice was always right. The only thing she had never managed to do was to get Sol to marry her officially.

At first Sol had gone back home regularly but, after he had taken the money trunks from the old cabin to his house at Okeechobee, his trips there became rare. In the last two years Clayton had left the grove and was replaced by a man called Donovan, who Sol had hired by mail.

The war in Europe was one of the reasons for stepping up the production of the fields. Sol had registered for the army but was told his job supplying food was far more important to the war than just being one more soldier. So he took the work seriously.

When Sol drove off the main road, he was not sure if it was the right way. So much looked different. The place where the pen had been was now more rows of orange trees. As he drove further, he became more perplexed. More orange trees stood where the hammock used to be.

Then he saw, right in the middle of two rows of trees, five stones, all with the name MacIvey. He stared for a moment, and then realized what had been done. He screamed furiously, "Damn you! Damn you, you son of a bitch! I'll kill you!"

When Bonnie heard him, she was frightened. Sol started the car and soon they arrived at a small clearing containing a new house and two cabins.

A cloud of dust came up as Sol jumped from the car and grabbed a Winchester from the back seat. Tim and Jessie ran from one cabin. Jessie was crying and Tim said, "I couldn't stop him, Mister Sol! I tried, but he wouldn't listen to me!"

Donovan came from the house. He was a huge man, built like an ox. Sol pointed the Winchester at him and said, "I'm going to blow your head off, you no good bastard!"

Donovan froze, looking at the trembling hand on the trigger. He spoke as calmly as possible. "You must be Mister Sol. Why are you so upset? I was hired to run the grove, not to look after some old huts and run an old-folks home. And I've made a good profit for you. You should be glad I cleared all that stuff and grew more oranges."

Bonnie had never seen Sol so angry, and she knew what he was going to do. She ran to him and shouted, "Please, Sol, don't! What's done is done, and killing him won't bring it back! It'll only bring trouble!"

He looked at her terrified face, then back at Donovan, and then he said, "I want you to get off this place in ten minutes! If you are still here then, so help me God, I'll kill you!"

Within minutes Donovan and his wife left the house and disappeared on horseback into the woods.

When Sol had calmed down, he made Tim the new manager and promised to hire some more men to work in the fields.

Then he got into the car and drove off. When he reached the place where the cow pen had been, he stopped and cried.

Bonnie put her arms around him and he controlled himself. "You know Bonnie, that bastard bulldozed two whole lifetimes. Everything Pappa and Grampy did is gone now."

Sol was shocked as he suddenly understood why Toby had been so angry when he destroyed the forest, a place that both Zech and Toby had loved. To them it was much more than just another swamp and forest. And he had done the same thing Donovan had done, only for vegetables rather than oranges.

He wiped his eyes and said, "They'll never forgive me for this, Bonnie, and I know I won't forgive myself. All they left behind is gone now, and regrets won't bring it back. Toby was right and I was wrong, but it's done now, and what's done can't be undone. I guess nothing in this whole damned stinking world lasts forever."

None of it made sense to her, she didn't even know who Toby was, and her puzzled expression stayed on her face as he started he car and they drove off together.

THIRTY-THREE

1924

After moving to Okeechobee Sol made many trips to Miami. The remote town of the early 1900 had changed a lot. Flagler's railroad had brought people, and people from everywhere were buying land like mad in the area.

In January of 1912 Sol and Bonnie went with the first train from Miami to Key West. The whole island was a big party such as neither of them had ever seen. Rum flowed like coconut milk. There was dancing in the streets, and outdoor tables were filled with meals of exotic fish. They were both tired when they arrived back in Miami and then returned gladly to their remote home.

Sol had also visited his property at Miami Beach for the first time. The other properties were developing at high speed. But not his land, and developers were searching intensively for the owner, a MacIvey family with the address "Kissimmee wilderness".

After the war ended, the construction activity increased very fast, and then thousands of tourists came into the area, wanting to see or own a piece of this tropical paradise.

Sol and Bonnie watched the development and waited, knowing that with each day his property was becoming more valuable.

In 1923 he made the first move, hiring a contractor to build a house with an office. Inside Sol had one room with thick concrete walls and iron bars across each window. This was the place where he stored all his money because he still had not used any bank account and was pleased that he had followed the system of his father and grandfather. As soon as the house was finished, he hired a foreman for the vegetable business and set off with Bonnie to take part in the great Florida Boom. The sign outside his office read: "MacIvey Real Estate and Development Company."

When Sol started to study the current prices, he and Bonnie decided to take the first step. He went to a small printing shop and ordered leaflets saying MacIvey Real Estate would be selling good land beginning at 8 a.m. the next morning, first come first served. He and Bonnie handed out the leaflets all over Miami and Miami Beach.

The next morning they did not know what to expect. But when Sol opened the door there was a line of people outside, waiting impatiently in the heat.

By noon they had sold a lot of land and made $850,000 in cash. This boom went on for months. And by that time Bonnie and Sol were exhausted and they decided to spend several months in their Okeechobee home. They had made a fortune of $80 million which was lying in their Miami safe.

THIRTY-FOUR

September 15
1928

Sol and Bonnie had left Miami to escape the memories of the great devastation when the September hurricane had almost destroyed all the area, bringing an end to the land boom.

Both had survived the storm in their little concrete fortress, but almost all other houses, hotels and office buildings had been flattened to the ground, and the dreams and hopes of thousands of people swept away.

Sol and Bonnie had not been not at all hurt by it. In fact, they had even profited. A week after the storm they had put up a sign in front of their office saying: "We're Buying". And they had the cash money to do so, paying five cents for flattened property. Sol had purchased property after property, believing that someday the area would recover again.

But they didn't want to witness another Miami-style hurricane and drove to their home at Lake Okeechobee which they thought would protect them from the next storm that was meant to roll over southern Florida.

The sun did not come up the next morning. At first the wind banged against the side of the house. The wind became stronger and frightening. Sol nailed all the doors and windows shut and saw that his car had been blown away.

"I'm afraid, Sol. Really afraid!" Bonnie shouted. "What are we going to do?"

Later that day they stared with horror as the water of the lake covered the floor, rising rapidly. Sol worked hard make a rescue platform out of bits of furniture. Both of them climbed onto it, hugging each other as pieces of the house gave way and sailed off like leaves, exposing them to the heavy rain that made breathing almost impossible.

And then it suddenly stopped, as if someone had switched off a light. Sol looked up through the hole in the roof, seeing moon and stars, one big circle of peaceful sky. He said, "It's the eye, Bonnie. The storm's passing over us now. It will come again, but we'll make it. I'll hold you."

With fear in her eyes Bonnie said, "Sol, I might as well say it now as ever. I love you. But we should have been married. I don't want to die in sin. Say you love me. If you tell me now, it'll be all right."

Sol pulled her closer, feeling her tremble. "I do love you, Bonnie, and always have. The first thing we'll do when this is over is look for a preacher. No other MacIvey before me ran away from the one they loved, and I won't any longer. I declare you right before God to be my wife. And tomorrow we'll have a preacher say the words."

She kissed him. "Thanks, darling. That's what I wanted you to say. I can face it now. I think I'll be forgiven."

And then the sky exploded, with a sound like dynamite, sending boards and beams and window frames flying away with the howling wind. Sol felt himself ripped from Bonnie and flipped over and over like a coin, splashing down into angry, boiling water, gasping for breath as he went under and came back again, finally locking his arms onto a section of roof as it swept by. His shouts of "Bonnie ...!

Bonnie ...!" were heard only by himself as he moved rapidly over what had once been a vegetable field.

Dawn came from a sky still gray, but the violence was gone. Sol pushed away from the beams and pulled himself slowly up the muddy bank. He looked around; no tree was left standing, no house or barn, nothing visible but water, and the floating bodies of dead animals and humans. He cried out, "Bonnie ...! Where are you, Bonnie?"

Suddenly he stopped and shook his fist at the gray clouds covering the sky. "Damn you! Damn you! You'll not do this again! We'll dyke the lake so you can't do it again! Bonnie ... Answer me, Bonnie ...!"

But there was no answer, and there never would be. Bonnie was among the two thousand people who died and had vanished forever.

THIRTY-FIVE

Miami
1954

Sol sat behind his mahogany desk in his office at the top floor of the MacIvey State Bank. A young reporter was sitting opposite him, saying, "I'm Alice Bryant, Mister MacIvey. I've always wanted to meet you but never thought I would. And I want to congratulate you on the honor of being selected "Citizen of the Year" for your lifetime contribution to the Miami area and to Florida."

"Just what is it you want to know?" Sol asked, already bored as he leaned back in the chair.

"Oh, just everything," she replied happily. "Something about your family background, how you got started, where you went to school. All that sort of thing."

Sol told his story with a smile. "My granddaddy was a plantation owner in Georgia and came to Florida before the Civil War to establish a cattle and orange grove empire. He served as a Confederate general during the war. My pappa helped Grampy buy the land and start business. I learned from them. Before I took it over, I was sent away to college. Graduated from the University of Virginia in 1906, magna cum laude ..."

The Okeechobee hurricane of 1928 changed the face of the land forever. As Sol had decided that morning at the canal, the lake was dyked. Canals were cut into the ground, drying up the soil and turning the life-giving water away from the Big Cypress Swamp and the Everglades. It caused serious droughts in dry seasons. It was all done with good intentions at the time, but it still created a change of nature that could never be changed back.

Sol played a big part in it because of his anger at the storm and Bonnie's death. He rebuilt the Okeechobee house, this time of concrete and steel, and then went back to Miami. When the Depression came in 1929, causing banks to fail, he started his own bank with hard cash from his private vault.

During World War II he became chairman of war bond drives and donated money to the United Service Organizations, and later on gave to lots of charities.

After the war, another boom started, not quite as strong as the last one but a boom nevertheless. But Sol was no longer an active part of it, turning the management of MacIvey Development over to eager young executives he hired; but before he realized what was happening he had created a monster that would not stop until the last swamp was drained, and the last tree cut.

In 1952 he built his hotel, naming it La Florida, twenty-five stories of concrete and glass overlooking the ocean on Miami Beach. But more and more he retreated into his private world.

Sol sat at the head table, looking out at a sea of faces he did not know and did not want to know. His red hair was now sandy gray, but his body was still lean. He was dressed in a black suit just made for this occasion.

Finally, the evening came to the climax as a man spoke loudly into the microphone. Sol did not listen to his words, knowing already what would be said about him. After the closing words he got up to the thunderous applause and made his way to the podium. He adjusted the mike; then he spoke slowly and deliberately,

"All that stuff you just heard about me is pure shit. It's all lies I made up just to see how gullible you are. And it's all a shame on the name of MacIvey. To all those MacIveys who left this earth before me, I apologize for telling such lies."

He paused and looked out over an audience now shocked into silence, and then he continued, telling his life story and about the hard existences of the MacIveys and their fight against nature and life.

"My grampy would never buy the land and never owned so much as a grain of sand. He believed that no man can own the land, that it all belongs to the Lord, and the Lord lets us stay on it temporarily as tenants. If this is so, and I now believe it's so, then the Lord must be powerful mad at all of us for what we've done to His property. There'll be a day of reckoning for you and for me.

"It wasn't me who, as was said, "conquered the wilderness". I am the least of the MacIveys. It was Tobias MacIvey and Emma and Skillit and Zech and Glenda and Frog and Bonzo and several others. All I did was cash in on what they did.

"The ones who got the down-side from all this so-called "progress" were an old man named Keith Tiger and Tawanda Cypress and my half-brother Toby Cypress MacIvey and a bunch more still living out there in the swamps in chickees.

"When I first started out alone after pappa died, I didn't know what I was doing, and I thought I was doing the right thing. But you sons a' bitches knew, and you did it deliberately. That's the only thing that marks me from you. The reason with me is stupidity. With you it's greed. More is better, bigger is better. Well, you bastards are too stupid to know there soon won't be no more.

"All of you who don't like what I've said here tonight can kiss my ass. You've seen the last of me you'll ever see. I'm going to hide from such as you and pray for forgiveness for what I've helped do. If I could rip out the concrete and put back the woods, I would. But I can't. From what we've done to this place in just the past fifty years, what the hell you think it's going to be like in another fifty?"

He stopped abruptly, stepped back and said, "I do thank you kindly for your attention." Then he walked quickly to the nearest exit and left.

Vocabulary

abruptly [ə'brʌptli] plötzlich
absence ['æbsəns] Abwesenheit
(to) **accept** [ək'sept] annehmen
acre ['ɑːftəlaɪf] Acre
afterlife ['ɑːftəlaɪf] Jenseits
(to) **aim** [eɪm] zielen auf
ain't [eɪnt] *umg.* isn't
alligator [ælɪge] Alligator
anger ['æŋgə] Groll, Ärger
applause [ə'plɔːz] Applaus
armed [ɑːmd] bewaffnet
ass [æs] *umg.* Arsch
attention [ə'tenʃn] Aufmerksamkeit
awake [ə'weɪk] wach
(to) **awaken** [ə'weɪkən] aufwachen
axe [æks] Axt
backward ['bækwəd] rückwärts
bandage ['bændɪdʒ] bandagieren
bang [bæŋ] Knall
bank account ['bæŋk əkaʊnt] Bankkonto
barely ['beəli] gerade noch
barn [bɑːn] Scheune
barrel ['bærəl] Fass
bastard ['bɑːstəd] Bastard
battle ['bætl] Kampf
beam [biːm] Balken
beard [bɪəd] Bart
beehive [biːhaɪv] Bienenstock
beer [bɪə] Bier
beholden [bɪ'həʊldən] dankbar
(to) **bellow** ['beləʊ] brüllen
belly ['beli] Bauch
belt [belt] Gürtel
bench [bentʃ] Bank
berry ['beri] Beere
(to) **bite** [baɪt] beißen
blacksmith ['blæksmɪθ] Schmied
blade (of a knife) [bleɪd (əv ə naɪf)] Klinge eines Messers
blinding ['blaɪndɪŋ] blendend
(to) **blink** [blɪŋk] blinken
blizzard ['blɪzəd] Schneesturm
blossom ['blɒsəm] Blüte
bonus ['bəʊnəs] Bonus
bony ['bəʊni] knochig
boom [buːm] Bumm (knallendes Geräusch)
(to) **bounce** [baʊns] abprallen, hüpfen, aufspringen
(to) **bow** [baʊ] beugen
bow [bəʊ] Bogen
brain [breɪn] Gehirn
branch [brɑːntʃ] Zweig
(to) **brand** [brænd] markieren
branding iron ['brændɪŋ,aɪən] Brandeisen
breath [breθ] Atem
breathless ['breθləs] atmenlos
brilliant ['brɪliənt] glänzend
brush [brʌʃ] Dickicht
bud [bʌd] Knospe
(to) **bulldoze** ['bʊldəʊz] (planieren) dem Erdboden gleichmachen
bullet ['bʊlɪt] Munition

bunch [bʌntʃ] Bündel, Haufen, Strauß
bushwhacking [bʊʃ'wækɪŋ] Auflauern
buzzard ['bʌzəd] Bussard
(to) **calculate** ['kælkjʊleɪt] (aus)rechnen
calf [kɑːf] Kalb
cash [kæʃ] Bargeld
celery ['seləri] Sellerie
ceremony ['serəməni] Zeremonie
chain [tʃeɪn] Kette (Spülung ziehen)
chairman ['tʃeəmən] Vorsitzender der Kriegsanleihe
chest [tʃest] Brust
chickee ['tʃɪki] Hütte eines amerikanischen Ureinwohners
childbirth ['tʃaɪldbɜːθ] Entbindung
chore [tʃɔː] lästige Arbeit/ Hausarbeit
chunk [tʃʌŋk] Stück
citizen ['sɪtɪzn] Bürger
clearing ['klɪərɪŋ] Waldlichtung
cloth [klɒθ] Stoff
coffin ['kɒfɪn] Sarg
(to) **complain** [kəm'pleɪn] klagen, jammern
(to) **confess** [kən'fes] zugeben
(to) **congratulate** [kən'grætʃuleɪt] gratulieren
conquer ['kɒŋkə] erobern
constantly ['kɒnstəntli] ständig
construction [kən'strʌkʃn] Bau
(to) **contain** [kən'teɪn] enthalten
contractor [kən'træktə] Auftragnehmer
contribution [kən'trɪbjətə] Beitrag
(to) **convince** [kən'vɪns] überzeugen
cooking pot ['kʊkɪŋ pɒt] Kochtopf
(to) **crack a whip** [kræk ə wɪp] eine Peitsche knallen lassen
(to) **crawl** [krɔːl] krabbeln
(to) **crush** [krʌʃ] zerstören
cucumber ['kjuːkʌmbə] Gurke
curiously ['kjʊəriəsli] seltsamerweise
current ['kʌrənt] gegenwärtig
customer ['kʌstəmə] Kunde
cypress tree ['saɪprəs triː] Zypresse
dammit ['dæmɪt] *umg.* verdammt
damned [dæmd] *umg.* verdammt
darkness ['dɑːknəs] Dunkelheit
day of reckoning [deɪ əv 'rekənɪŋ] Tag der Abrechnung
(to) **declare** [dɪ'kleə] feststellen
deed [diːd] Vertrag
deliberately [dɪ'lɪbərətli] absichtlich
denim ['denɪm] Jeansstoff
dense [dens] dicht
depression [dɪ'preʃn] Despression
deserter [dɪ'zɜːtə] Fahnenflüchtiger
devastation [ˌdevə'steɪʃn] Verwüstung

development [dɪ'veləpmənt] Entwicklung
devil ['devl] Teufel
difficulty ['dɪfɪkəlti] Schwierigkeit
directly [də'rektli] gerade
dock [dɒk] Hafenanlage
doorman ['dɒːmən] Türsteher
(to) **drag** [dræg] nachschleppen
drain [dreɪn] ablaufen lassen
dried [draɪd] getrocknet
driveway ['draɪvweɪ] Fahrweg
drone [drəʊn] Dröhnen
drought [draʊt] Dürre
drover ['drəʊvər] Viehhändler
(to) **dry up** [ˌdraɪ'ʌp] austrocknen
dump [dʌmp] *umg.* Bruchbude
dyke [daɪk] Damm
dynamite ['daɪnəmaɪt] Dynamit
eager ['iːgə] eifrig
edge [edʒ] Rand
elegant ['elɪgənt] elegant
error ['erə] Fehler
(to) **establish** [ɪ'stæblɪʃ] etablieren
excitement [ɪk'saɪtmənt] Aufregung
(to) **exclaim** [ɪk'skleɪm] ausstoßen, schreien
executive [ɪg'zekjətɪv] Direktor
exhausted [ɪg'zɔːstɪd] erschöpft
existence [ɪg'zɪstəns] Existenz
exit ['eksɪt] Ausgang
exotic [ɪg'zɒtɪk] exotisch
(to) **explode** [ɪk'spləʊd] explodieren
(to) **expose** [ɪk'spəʊz] aufdecken
extensive [ɪk'stensɪv] erheblich
(to) **fail** [feɪl] Bankrott gehen
(to) **faint** [feɪnt] ohnmächtig werden
faint [feɪnt] matt
fantasy ['fæntəsi] Fantasie
farewell [ˌfeə'wel] Abschied
farmland ['fɑːmlænd] Ackerland
fascination [ˌfæsɪ'neɪʃn] Faszination
(to) **fear** [fɪə] fürchten
fearsome [fɪəsəm] fürchterlich
feebly ['fiːbli] schwach
fellow ['feləʊ] Kerl
(to) **fire (a gun)** ['faɪə (ə gʌn)] schießen
fireplace ['faɪəpleɪs] Kamin
firewood ['faɪəwʊd] Brennholz
firmly [fɜːmli] fest
(to) **flatten** ['flætn] plätten
(to) **float** [fləʊt] flößen
flood [flʌd] Flut
flour ['flaʊə] Mehl
flowerbed ['flaʊəbed] Blumenbeet
(to) **fool** [fuːl] betrügen
foreman ['fɔːmən] Aufseher
forgiveness [fə'gɪvnɪs] Vergebung
fortress ['fɔːtrəs] Zitadelle
frame [freɪm] Rahmen
(to) **freeze** [friːz] einfrieren
frustrated [frʌ'streɪtɪd] frustriert
fur [fɜː] Pelz
furious ['fjʊəriəs] wütend
further ['fɜːðə] weiter
(to) **gallop** ['gæləp] galoppieren
gang [gæŋ] Gruppe

(to) **gasp** [gɑːsp] japsen
'gator ['geɪtəʳ] *umg.* Alligator
gladly ['glædli] freudig
glare [gleə] Blendlicht
glowing ['gləʊɪŋ] glühend
God a'mighty [gɒd ɔː'maɪti] *umg.* Oh Gott!
goddam ['gɒddæm] *umg.* gottverdammt
gonna ['gənə, 'gɒnə] *umg.* going to
grain [greɪn] Korn
grave [greɪv] Grab
(to) **graze** [greɪz] grasen
greed [griːd] Gier
greens [griːnz] *umg.* Gemüse
(to) **grin** [grɪn] grinsen
grove [grəʊv] Baumgruppe
(to) **growl** [graʊl] knurren
guilt [gɪlt] Schuld
gullible ['gʌləbl] leichtgläubig
gunman ['gʌnmən] Bewaffneter
gunslinger ['gʌnslɪŋəʳ] Revolverheld
half-breed ['hɑːfˌbriːd] Halbblut
halfway [ˌhɑːf'weɪ] halbwegs
hammer ['hæmə] Hammer
hammock ['hæmək] kleiner Hügel
handful ['hændfʊl] Handvoll
hardly ['hɑːdli] kaum
harm [hɑːm] Leid
harshly [hɑːʃli] rau
heavy ['hevi] schwer
herd [hɜːd] Herde
(to) **hesitate** ['hezɪteɪt] zaudern
hesitation [ˌhezɪ'teɪʃn] Zögern
(to) **hire** ['haɪə] anstellen
homestead ['həʊmsted] Bauernhof
honey ['hʌni] Honig
hood [hʊd] Kappe
hoof [huːf] Huf
horn [hɔːn] Horn
horseback ['hɔːsbæk] zu Pferde
hostility [hɒ'stɪləti] Feindseligkeit
housekeeper ['haʊskiːpə] Haushälter/in
howl [haʊl] Schrei
hurricane ['hʌrɪkən] Hurrikan
(to) **increase** [ɪn'kriːs] mehren
inland ['ɪnlənd] Landesinnere
(to) **insist** [ɪn'sɪst] beharren
(to) **inspect** [ɪn'spekt] überprüfen
intensively [ɪn'tensɪvli] intensiv, eingehend
(to) **interfere** [ˌɪntə'fɪə] einmischen
interior [ɪn'tɪəriə] Innere
iron ['aɪən] Eisen
isolated ['aɪsəleɪtɪd] isoliert
judgement ['dʒʌdʒmənt] Beurteilung
Kissimmee [kɪs'sɪmiː] ein Fluß in Südflorida
lagoon [lə'guːn] Lagune
lard [lɑːd] Schmalz
(to) **last** [lɑːst] andauern
leaflet ['liːflət] Broschüre
lean [liːn] schlank
length [leŋθ] Länge
lifestyle ['laɪfstaɪl] Lebensstil
lifetime ['laɪftaɪm] Lebenszeit
lightning ['laɪtnɪŋ] Blitz, blitzen
limp [lɪmp] hinken

loose [luːs] frei
Lordy ['lɔːdi] Großer Gott!
lover ['lʌvə] Geliebte(r)
low [ləʊ] tief
mahogany [mə'hɒgəni] Mahogani
marsh [mɑːʃ] Marsch
marshal ['mɑːʃl] Polizeidirektor
marshtackie [mɑːʃ'tæki] amerikanische Pferdrasse
meanwhile ['miːnwaɪl] währenddessen
medicine ['medsn] Medikament
(to) **melt** [melt] abschmelzen
memory ['meməri] Gedächtnis
(to) **mention** ['menʃn] erwähnen
midnight ['mɪdnaɪt] Mitternacht
miscarriage ['mɪskærɪdʒ] Fehlgeburt
Miss ['mɪs] Fräulein
Mister ['mɪstə] Herr
(to) **moan** [məʊn] stöhnen
mostly ['məʊstli] meistens
mound [maʊnd] Hügel
(to) **mount** [maʊnt] aufsitzen
mournfully ['mɔːnfəli] trauervoll
multicoloured [ˌmʌlti'kʌləd] mehrfarbig
(to) **mutter** ['mʌtə] murmeln
nail [neɪl] nageln
negro ['niːgrəʊ] *(veraltet)* Neger
neither … nor ['naɪðə^{r} … nɔː^{r}] weder … noch
nevertheless [ˌnevəðə'les] trotzdem
nigger ['nɪgə^{r}] *(beleidigend)* Neger
noon [nuːn] Mittag
objection [əb'dʒekʃn] Widerspruch
occasion [ə'keɪʒn] Ereignis
oil [ɔɪl] Öl
overalls ['əʊvərɔːlz] Latzhose
(to) **overlook** [ˌəʊvə'lʊk] überschauen
overnight [ˌəʊvə'naɪt] über Nacht
(to) **overwhelm** [ˌəʊvə'welm] überschwemmen
ox [ɒks] Ochse
palm tree ['pɑːm triː] Palme
pasture ['pɑːstʃə] Viehweide
peaceful ['piːsfl] friedlich
perfection [pə'fekʃn] Perfektion
permanent ['pɜːmənənt] permanent
perplexed [pə'plekst] ratlos
(to) **plant** [plɑːnt] anpflanzen
pleasantly ['pleznt] erfreulich
podium ['pəʊdɪəm] Podium
poorly ['pɔːli, 'pʊəli] schlecht
porch [pɔːtʃ] Veranda
(to) **pour** [pɔː] eingießen
powerless ['paʊələs] machtlos
preacher ['priːtʃə] Prediger
pregnant ['pregnənt] schwanger
(to) **press** [pres] drücken
pride [praɪd] Stolz
process ['prəʊses] Ablauf
product ['prɒdʌkt] Produkt
production [prə'dʌkʃn] Ertrag
(to) **profit** ['prɒfɪt] profitieren
property ['prɒpəti] Eigentum
protection [prə'tekʃn] Schutz
(to) **purchase** ['pɜːtʃəs] kaufen
pure [pjʊə] rein

raccoon [rə'kuːn] Waschbär
railroad ['reɪlrəʊd] Eisenbahn
rainstorm ['reɪnˌstɔːm] Regenguss
rancher ['rɑːntʃə] Viehzüchter
rawhide ['rɔːˌhaɪd] Rohleder
real estate ['rɑːntʃə] Immobilien
rear [rɪə] Rückseite
(to) **rebuild** [ˌriː'bɪld] umbauen
(to) **refuse** [ˌriː'bɪld] ablehnen
(to) **register** ['redʒɪstə] einschreiben
(to) **regret** [rɪ'gret] bereuen
(to) **remain** [rɪ'meɪn] bleiben
(to) **remind** [rɪ'maɪnd] erinnern
(to) **remote** [rɪ'məʊt] abgelegen
(to) **respond** [rɪ'spɒnd] antworten
(to) **retreat** [rɪ'triːt] zurücktreten
(to) **return** [rɪ'tɜːn] zurückkehren
rider ['raɪdə] Reiter
rifle ['raɪfl] Gewehr, Büchse
(to) **rip** [rɪp] reißen
risk [rɪsk] riskieren
roadblock ['rəʊdblɒk] Staßensperre
(to) **roast** [rəʊst] braten
root [ruːt] Wurzel
rotgut ['rɒtˌgʌt] Fusel
rough [rʌf] gemein
(to) **round up** [ˌraʊnd'ʌp] zusammentreiben
rum [rʌm] Rum
(to) **rush** [rʌʃ] hasten
rustler ['rʌslə˞] Viehdieb
sack [sæk] Sack
(to) **saddle** ['sædl] satteln
saloon [sə'luːn] Saloon
satisfaction [ˌsætɪs'fækʃn] Befriedigung
(to be) **scared** (of sth.) (vor etwas) Angst haben
(to) **scramble** ['skræmbl] drängen
(to) **scratch** [skrætʃ] kratzen
scrub [skrʌb] Buschwerk
seed [siːd] Saatgut
(to) **select** [sɪ'lekt] auswählen
Seminole ['seməˌnəʊl] Indianervolk in Amerika
sense [sens] Sinn
shame [ʃeɪm] Scham
sharply ['ʃɑːpli] scharf
shed [ʃed] Hütte
shelter ['ʃeltə] Unterkunft
shore [ʃɔː] Ufer
shortly after ['ʃɔːtli 'ɑːftə] kurz danach
shotgun ['ʃɒtgʌn] Schrotflinte, Jagdgewehr
shovel ['ʃʌvl] Schippe
(to) **sigh** [saɪ] seufzen
signal ['sɪgnəl] Signal
silence ['saɪləns] Ruhe
similar ['sɪmələ] ähnlich
sin [sɪn] Sünde
site [saɪt] Ort
slim [slɪm] schlank
(to) **slip** [slɪp] ausrutschen
smokehouse ['sməʊkˌhaʊs] Räucherkammer
(to) **snap** [snæp] schnappen
sniff [snɪf] an etw. riechen
solid ['sɒlɪd] fest
someday ['sʌmdeɪ] eines Tages

son of a bitch ['sʌnəvə,bɪtʃ] *umg.* Mistkerl
specialist ['speʃəlɪst] Facharzt
(to) **squeak** [skwiːk] kreischen
stable [skwiːk] Stall
stale [steɪl] abgestanden
(to) **stamp** [stæmp] stampfen
state [steɪt] Staat
step [step] einen Schritt tun, treten
stewed [stjuːd] geschmort
storefront ['stɔː,frʌnt] Fassade
storeroom ['stɔːruːm] Lagerhalle
stove [stəʊv] Heizofen
stovepipe ['stəʊv,paɪp] Ofenrohr
stubborn ['stʌbən] störrisch
(to) **stumble** ['stʌmbl] stolpern
stupidity [stjuː'pɪdəti] Dummheit
(to) **suggest** [sə'dʒest] empfehlen
suit [suːt] Anzug
supplier [sə'plaɪə] Lieferer
supplies [sə'plaɪz] Lieferungen
(to) **supply** [sə'plaɪ] liefern
surface ['sɜːfɪs] Oberfläche
swamp [swɒmp] Sumpf
swarm [swɔːm] Schwarm
sweaty ['sweti] verschwitzt
(to) **switch on** [,swɪtʃ'ɒn] anmachen
temporarily [,tempə'rərɪli] temporär
tenant ['tenənt] Mieter
thankful ['θæŋkfl] dankbar
thick [θɪk] dicht
thunder ['θʌndə] Donner
thunderous ['θʌnderəs] donnernd
tiny ['taɪni] winzig
torch [tɔːtʃ] Fackel
traitor ['treɪtə] Verräter
(to) **tremble** ['trembl] zittern
trial and error ['traɪəl ənd 'erə] Versuch und Irrtum
trigger ['trɪgə] Abzug
tropical ['trɒpɪkl] tropisch
trunk [trʌŋk] Koffer, Kiste
truth [truːθ] Wahrheit
unable [ʌn'eɪbl] unfähig
unborn [,ʌn'bɔːn] ungeboren
unsteadily [ʌn'stedili] wackelig
upward ['ʌpwəd] aufwärts
in vain [(ɪn) veɪn] vergeblich
(to) **vanish** ['vænɪʃ] verschwinden
varmint ['vɑːmɪnt] Schädling
vast [vɑːst] rießig
vault [vɔːlt] Tresorraum
vegetation [,vedʒə'teɪʃn] Vegetation
visible ['vɪzəbl] sichtbar
wagon ['wægən] Wagen
waitress ['weɪtrəs] Kellnerin
waterfront ['wɔːtəfrʌnt] Hafenviertel
wedding ['wedɪŋ] Hochzeit
What the hell ...? [,wɒt ðə'hel] *umg.* Was zum Teufel ...?
whip [wɪp] Peitsche
(to) **whip** [wɪp] jmd. versohlen
(to) **widen** ['waɪdn] breiter werden
wilderness ['wildənəs] Wildnis
willing ['wɪlɪŋ] willig
wooden ['wʊdn] hölzern

Questions and Tasks

ONE

Q1 Why did the MacIveys leave Georgia?

Q2 What food did the MacIveys have to begin with?

Q3 What were the main dangers for the MacIveys in the wilderness?

TWO

Q1 Why did the white men treat the Indians so cruelly?

Q2 How did Tobias help the Indians?

Q3 What did Tobias need to start collecting cattle?

THREE

Q1 How did Tobias have to help the state marshal?

Q2 Why did the drivers let the cows walk slowly?

Q3 How did the men protect the cattle from wolves?

T1 Write Emma's diary entry for the day of the bear attack.

FOUR

Q1 Why did Tobias think he had the right to take the dead soldier's belongings?

Q2 What happened to Emma and Zech while Tobias was away?

Q3 Why did Tobias decide to go further south?

FIVE

Q1 Why wasn't an army horse any good for catching cows?

Q2 Why do you think they had to brand the cow?

T1 Find some information about the American Civil War. Who were the Confederates?

SIX

Q1 What did the Indians teach Tobias and Zech about cow hunting?

Q2 The horse and the dogs "mean more than you know" to Tobias. Why?

SEVEN

Q1 What new strategy did Tobias and Zech use to collect cows?

Q2 How did Tobias react when he and Zech met Skillit?

EIGHT

Q1 Describe Skillit's life before and after the war. How did it change?

Q2 Why did Skillit decide to stay with the MacIvey family?

T1 What can you find out about the men "dressed in white sheets"?

NINE

Q1 What sign showed that danger was approaching the MacIveys?

Q2 How does the author describe the rain?

Q3 Why did Emma believe the storm killed their cows?

T1 Explore why Florida has so much rain? What are the dangers today? What is the reason for the increasing danger of extreme weather conditions?

TEN

Q1 What was the next new tactic to catch cows?

Q2 Do you think that the two men will be helpful for Tobias? Explain why or why not.

T1 Draw and write an advertisement for a new driver that Tobias – if he had been able to write - could have fixed to a tree.

ELEVEN

Q1 Why were people selling cows to drivers?

Q2 What did the men do to save the herd from the wolves?

Q3 What does the author compare the alligator attack to?

TWELVE

Q1 What did Tobias do with the first money he got?

Q2 Why didn't Tobias want a drink of rum?

Q4 What was so strange about the drivers that the ferryman compared them to a circus?

THIRTEEN

Q1 What did Tobias start doing apart from collecting cows?

Q3 How did Tobias do with his money?

Q3 Was it worth leaving the cows to go into town? What might have happened if they had not left?

Q4 Summarize the lesson that Tobias wanted to teach Zech. Do you agree?

T1 If Zech could have written, what letter would he have written to Glenda after coming home?

FOURTEEN

Q1 What should Tobias have done to prevent the hanging of the Indian boys?

Q2 Why do you think Tobias decided to buy so many Winchesters?

Q3 Why did the white cowboys think that the cows were stolen?

FIFTEEN

Q1 Why do you think Tobias didn't tell Tony the truth right away?

Q2 Why were the Winchesters good for the Indians?

Q3 What was so impressive about Tawanda?

Q4 What did Tobias try to tell Zech about relationships with girls?

T1 Imagine Zech telling his story about their stay with the Indians to his mother. Write what you think he would have said.

SIXTEEN

Q1 What did Zech like and what didn't he like about the Christmas celebrations in Fort Drum?

Q2 What do you think of Glenda's way to "get promised"?

Q3 Zech had a dilemma: Which girl might be best for him? What would you advise? Why?

SEVENTEEN

Q1 What is the advantage of the orange business in comparison to herding cows?

Q2 Comment on Glenda's school education. What do you think this meant at that time?

Q3 What important step does Zech take to save the MacIvey's property? Why?

EIGHTEEN

Q1 How did Glenda fit into the MacIvey family?

Q2 Do you think that the pregnant Glenda should go on a drive? Explain why or why not.

T1 Write Glenda's letter to one of her friends in Jacksonville about the wedding and her first days in the MacIvey family.

NINETEEN

Q1 What did Glenda enjoy at the beginning of the drive?

Q2 What did Zech learn after the shooting had ended?

Q3 Why was Emma so important in this scene?

TWENTY

Q1 What was the main job for the MacIveys now?

Q2 What shows that Tawanda really loved Zech?

Q3 Zech felt guilty when he left the Indian settlement. Explain his theory of the "two worlds".

TWENTY-ONE

Q1 What had Skillit done in Kissimmee?

Q2 What did Tobias mean when he said "It's breaking up, Emma")?

TWENTY-TWO

Q1 Why was everyone against Tobias going on further drives?

Q2 Why was Zech unsure about meeting Tawanda again?

Q3 What had Zech's son experienced as a "half-breed"?

Q4 How did Zech try to act like a father for Toby?

TWENTY-THREE

Q1 What do you think caused Emma's death?
Q2 What did Tobias blame himself for? Why?
T1 Characterize Emma as she appeared in the book until now.

TWENTY-FOUR

Q1 How did the MacIvey family change after Emma's death?
Q2 What happened to the fences? Why?
Q3 Why did Tobias leave the house in the freeze?
Q4 Explain why, after Tobias' death, "Zech sat on the edge of the bed feeling that a part of him had also died."

TWENTY-FIVE

Q1 What had happened to nature as a result of the freeze?
Q2 What did the Indians' visit show about their relationship with Tobias?
Q3 Why did Zech feel guilty when he heard about Tawanda's death?
T1 Write Zech's diary entry for the day he hears about Tawanda's death.

TWENTY-SIX

Q1 What was so impressive about The Royal Poinciana Hotel?
Q2 Why do you think the MacIveys didn't get a room in the hotel?
Q3 Why could they buy orange trees in Fort Dallas?

Q4 What was the name of the island that was bought for Sol?
T1 Find out who the man called Ed-son was.

TWENTY-SEVEN

Q1 What had become a threat to cattle ranchers?
Q2 Why didn't Sol obey his father's order to stay at home?
Q3 Why do you think the doctor was angry about Zech's idea to save his leg.
Q4 Sol met his brother in the Indian camp. Describe his different reactions.

TWENTY-EIGHT

Q1 Why was it so difficult to mark the bull?
Q2 Bigger, stronger, better – what was the price of success for Zech? Was it worth it?
Q3 Explain what Frog's last wish shows about his relation to the family.
T1 What do you think of Zech's advice for his son about loving women?

TWENTY-NINE

Q1 Seven years later a lot had changed in the MacIvey business. Describe the changes.
Q2 Did Zech die fighting or did he give up life gladly? What do you think?
T1 Write a newspaper article about Zech's life and death.

THIRTY

Q1 Why do you think that Sol <u>had</u> to leave?

THIRTY-ONE

Q1 What had to be done to change marshland into farmland?

Q2 Do you agree that Sol was a traitor to the wishes of his father?

Q3 Why was Sol shy when the waitress came to take his order?

THIRTY-TWO

Q1 Why do you think Sol didn't marry Bonnie?

Q2 Why did Sol become so furious when he got back to his childhood home?

Q3 What effect did Donavan's changes to the hammock have on Sol?

THIRTY-THREE

Q1 How had the remote area of Miami changed?

Q2 What happened to Sol's business life?

T1 Create a leaflet for Sol's offer of lots.

THIRTY-FOUR

Q1 What caused the end of the land boom?

Q2 Describe Sol's business tactics.

T1 The flooding is a historical event. Find out more information. What was done to nature after this catastrophe?

T2 Write a newspaper article about the Okeechobee disaster.

THIRTY-FIVE

Q1 Why do you think Sol told lies to the newspaper reporter?

Q2 Why was Sol able to "come back" into business after the depression?

Q3 Comment on Sol's speech to the rich and successful people of Miami.

T2 Can the "progress" around Lake Okeechobee be changed? Find information from the present day.